How the Great Comedy Writers Create Laughter

How the Great Comedy Writers Create Laughter

LARRY WILDE

nh Nelson-Hall
Chicago

Library of Congress Cataloging in Publication Data

Wilde, Larry.
　How the great comedy writers create laughter.

　Bibliography: p.
　Includes index.
　　1.　Humorists, American—Interviews.　2.　American wit
and humor—History and criticism.　3.　Wit and humor—
Authorship.　I.　Title.
PS438.W5　　　　817'.5'409　　　　　　76-771
ISBN 0-88229-491-1

To David Friedman, George S. Kaufman,
Nat Hiken, and the other great comedy
writers with that rare gift to create
the words that make us laugh.

Other Books by Larry Wilde

The Great Comedians
The Official Polish/Italian Joke Book
The Official Jewish/Irish Joke Book
The Official Virgins/Sex Maniacs Joke Book
The Official Black Folks/White Folks Joke Book
More Polish/Italian Jokes
The Official Democrats/Republicans Joke Book

CONTENTS

ACKNOWLEDGMENTS

I wish to express my deepest appreciation to the following folks without whose help this book could never have reached the printer, let alone the reader:

First and foremost, my gratitude to all the comedy writers who were kind enough to grant me interviews . . .

The personnel at the New York and Los Angeles public libraries . . .

And Judy Broom, Barbara Bragliardi, Shelley Baumsten, Patti Calhoun, Marti Jones, Milt Josefsberg, Tony Noice, Brad Radnitz, Cathy Deutsch . . .

A very extra special thanks to my wife, Maryruth . . .

and

To Jane Jordan Browne, who made it all happen.

The
BEGINNING

At your local library you are likely to find a fair selection of reading matter dealing with the dissection of humor. Educators, psychologists, and philosophers have been probing the anatomy of comedy ever since Aristophanes, Aristotle, and Plato applied their analytical minds to it.

Happily, there are even works examining the styles and techniques of the great comedians and how they go about the formidable task of making people laugh.

Yet, astonishing as it may seem, there is less than a fistful of volumes that delve into *the craft of creating comedy*. The shelves abound with textbooks and instruction manuals on how to write everything from short stories and novels to business letters and poetry. Why is comedy writing so shamefully neglected?

Admittedly comedy, more than any other form of writing, is intangible, elusive, and ephemeral. Nevertheless, jokes, sketches, scripts, and shows are produced every day for nightclubs, the stage, television, and motion pictures.

The work is accomplished mostly by a handful of highly skilled craftsmen, artisans who have developed this unique ability to feed the nation's insatiable appetite for laughter. Who are these humorous-verbiage technicians? What makes them tick? How did their work come into existence?

Comedy writing as a profession in America evolved over a long period of time. Like most occupations, it came into being out of necessity.

Basically, it began in the mid-nineteenth century with Mark Twain, Josh Billings, and Artemus Ward. These three master storytellers all caught the public's attention in the same way. They started their careers by producing humorous articles for newspapers and magazines and eventually published books.

But all achieved international fame on the lecture platform. For it was through this medium that each man delivered his own brand of humor, evoking guffaws with material *he had written for himself*.

There were other forms of *vocal* high jinks in those days, done mostly in the honky-tonks, showboats, carnivals, dime museums, and town halls. They consisted of comic dialogues and farcical and satirical songs, which were usually performed on stage between acts of serious opera.

From these beginnings came minstrel shows and burlesque. Yet it fell to a later type of variety entertainment called vaudeville to nurture comedy as we know it today.

Vaudeville—instituted in 1885 by Boston theater manager B. F. Keith—provided an opportunity for the specialty act. Here, performers who could make the crowd laugh were suddenly spotlighted, and thus was born a new breed of entertainers—the two-man comedy team. Harrigan and Hart, McIntyre and Heath, and Weber and Fields were a few of the favorites at that time.

Then in the early 1900s *stand-up* comedians began to arrive as idols of the public. These were brave souls who stood as individuals all alone in front of the audience, telling jokes or doing impressions. There now emerged such luminaries as Eddie Foy, W. C. Fields, Ed Wynn, Fred Allen, Will Rogers, and Bert Williams (the first great black comic).

By and large, these pioneers hatched their own jokes. Through years of trial and error they perfected routines for which they eventually became famous. The *writing* was done on stage while performing in front of an audience.

The silent screen buffoons—Buster Keaton, Fatty Arbuckle, Harold Lloyd, Charlie Chaplin, Laurel and Hardy, *et al.*—also invented their own comic devices. Working in this new medium, they improvised fresh situations and funny plots for each two-reeler. Fortunately, the movie clowns had the guidance and direction of Hal Roach and Mack Sennett, who are often regarded as the screen's first comedy writers.

A few joke dispensers contributed sketches and blackouts used by the comics in vaudeville and burlesque, but it wasn't until the golden age of radio that the gag writer came into his own.

All of a sudden Bob Hope, Jack Benny, George Burns and Gracie Allen, Eddie Cantor, "Amos 'n' Andy," Fred Allen, and the other jesters of the airwaves required an endless supply of quips for their weekly programs. Now the comedy writer was on his way to becoming the most sought-after creative specialist of the twentieth century.

By the time television became the prime medium of entertainment, jokesmithing had developed into an honorable but precarious profession. Salaries were good—some experts earned as much as $3,500 per week—but the capacity for concocting comedy was such an inexplicable talent that only a comparative few were capable of handling the assignment.*

And so the search was on—and still is—to find new talent with fresh ideas. Unfortunately, no classrooms or formal school programs teach the delicate knack of penning lines that evoke laughter. The rules and techniques—if any exist—are as hard to grasp as a goldfish in a bowl. On the succeeding pages, however, we will attempt to pinpoint some of the mechanics by examining the inner workings of the comedic mind.

The interviews in this book deal with the entire spectrum of comedy writing, from newspaper columns to gags to "sitcoms" to stage plays. All information is gathered directly from the world's most proficient practitioners of the art.

Enlightenment begins with Goodman Ace. "Everybody has his own idea of how a joke will get a laugh," he points out. "The basic rule is that it should be phrased correctly. A word out of place will spoil the whole joke." After lots of years, he says,

---

*"The Bob Hope Show" boasts the writer who has been employed the longest: Les White has been with the comedian since 1932. Five years after that, Norman Sullivan joined the staff. The producer and head writer, Mort Lachman, as well as Charlie Lee and Gig Henry, have been with Hope for twenty years or more.

"You learn to put the right word in the right place so that the rhythm is there, and the joke makes sense."

Mel Brooks talks about the *truth* in writing. "Instead of creating a mythical premise for a stupid joke," he explains, "I found playing off truth got the best results. Observe and slightly exaggerate, and you have comedy."

Bill Dana has standards by which he both lives and works. "I do not have a joke file," he confesses. "I want everything that comes out of my head to be fresh and new. I like to change with the times. I'm an observer of the passing scene. If I see something that strikes me funny, I make a note of it. A lot of times, things I think can be amplified into a screenplay will end up as a paragraph or one line in something I'll write."

Carl Reiner believes his development as a writer happened as a matter of course. "I think the craft of writing is intuitive. If you're somebody who walks through life *naturally* examing things—which is what I always did—you become aware. . . . Nobody taught me. Nobody sat me down and said, 'Hey, to have a good scene here, you have to build this. . . . I go by the seat of my pants."

"There are certain rules that I have," divulges Neil Simon. "This does not apply to everything, but it's getting either people, forces of opposite desires and opposite personalities, opposite characters, and putting them in contact with each other—in contrast with each other — and letting the sparks fly in what I like to consider an intolerable situation."

In trying to fathom the complexities of the comedy writers' psyches it becomes conclusively clear that they are not computer machines that spew forth clever witticisms by simply punching a button marked CREATE. Nor are they freaks, boobs, kooks, maniacs, nuts, or bolts. They are, however, hypersensitive, indulgent, indefatigable, disciplined, sentimental, highly intelligent, and well-educated individuals.

Their influence on society is immeasurable. They are the word-picture painters, grammar innovators, word coiners, phrase makers, colloquial-expression designers of our times.

Abe Burrows made one small step for man and one giant leap for fellow writers in stating, "I claim with comedy we make much more serious points that we do with anything that's supposed to be serious. A laugh is one of the most profound things that can happen to a human being. When you make a man laugh, you have evidently hit him right where he lives—deep. You've done something universal. You've moved him in an area that he probably didn't dare even think about, and he laughs explosively."

"One of my goals as a playwright of comedy," says Burrows, "is to send the audience out feeling complete—satisfied. . . . I like to send them out feeling better than when they came in."

To which Norman Lear adds: "We try to make every show a celebration of life. We try to do shows where people cheer, and where people yell, where they fight hard, they bed a lot . . . I would hope—at least that's the intention—that people turn off these shows and feel better for having seen them."

It is the author's intent that when you finish the last page between these covers, you too, will feel better. Possibly a little wiser. Certainly more understanding of this deceptive facility.

The purpose of this book is to shed light on the inscrutable and mysterious art of putting together words that get guffaws, to give insight and perhaps clarify the mechanics and techniques of the comedic craft. Here, for the first time in their own words, is how the great comedy writers create laughter.

Larry Wilde
Hollywood, California

Goodman
ACE

G oodman Ace was born in Kansas City, Missouri, on January 15, 1899. He started his professional writing career as a cub reporter on the *Kansas City Post* after editing his high school paper, studying journalism at Kansas City Junior College, and selling shoes.

Later promoted to drama, movie, and vaudeville critic for the paper, Ace quickly became infamous for his barbed, witty criticisms *(sample review:* "The settings were beautiful—both of them").

In 1927 he married Jane Sherwood, a high school sweetheart. The following year Ace inaugurated a fifteen-minute weekly radio program at ten dollars a show to supplement his newspaper income. To fill the time slot, Ace read the comics and broadcast parts of his daily column.

"Easy Aces" began to evolve one day when the performers on the following quarter-hour program failed to arrive at the station. Signaled to continue talking, Ace called in Jane, who was waiting outside, and they ad-libbed about the bridge game they had played the night before.

Response from listeners was so favorable the station gave the Aces a sponsored show heard three times weekly. As the program grew in stature, Ace gave up his newspaper duties. He and Jane moved to New York, and "Easy Aces" became a network feature, which Ace continued to write, produce, and direct.

Aside from its great public appeal, "Easy Aces" served as a prime example for other humorists. It was a peerless domestic situation comedy with two wonderful characters. Jane was the harebrained malapropist and unconscious comic. Goodman was the perfect straight man, the intellectual who nevertheless found himself involved in stupidities from which his wife had little or no difficulty extricating herself.

Jane's malapropisms soon became the show's stock in trade:

"She's putting on the rich."

"Familiarity breeds attempt."

"I couldn't get a wink of sleep. I tossed all night, first heads, then tails. I woke up this morning with the palms of my feet hanging over the side of the bed."

Such classic "Jane-isms" made "Easy Aces" consistently the funniest show on radio.

After seventeen years of "Easy Aces" (1928-1945) Ace turned to writing for others, first a radio program for Danny Kaye (1946) then "The Big Show" for Tallulah Bankhead (1950-1952). Milton Berle brought Ace into television in 1952, and he subsequently wrote for Perry Como (1955-1959) and "The Sid Caesar Show" (1963-1965).

Now Ace lives quietly in a New York midtown apartment. He keeps busy turning out high-priced comedy scripts as well as a weekly column for a national magazine. His books are *The Book of Little Knowledge, The Fine Art of Hypochondria or How Are You,* and *Ladies and Gentlemen, Easy Aces.*

As I knocked on the door of Goodman Ace's office overlooking Park Avenue in New York, I braced myself for a barrage of vituperative expletives that would dampen my enthusiasm for interviewing the legendary dean of American comedy writers.

Famous throughout the entertainment industry for his caustic comments, he had been crisp and businesslike on the telephone, and now I feared facing the man with the indifferent and dispassionate voice.

Manny Shure, Ace's secretary "for more years than I can remember," ushered me into the great man's inner office. Hunched at a small mahogany desk, he nodded for me to sit while he continued editing a piece he had just written.

His black-rimmed glasses accentuated his graying temples and gave him a youthful look that belied his seventy years. A rust-and-cream-colored tie hung loosely from the opened collar of his white oxford button-down shirt, which was tucked neatly into his light brown slacks.

In a moment, as he looked up and smiled while I prepared my trusty tape recorder, I knew my fears were groundless. Ace was uncommonly cooperative and during the conversation exuded great delight in recounting anecdotes from his illustrious career.

You began your writing career as a newspaper reporter. How did you learn the technique of joke construction?

That just comes from practice—lots of years of

practice. Right now it's a very fine art. You learn to put the right word in the right place so that the rhythm is there, and the joke makes sense. You can tell a joke to a layman, and he'll repeat it and tell it all wrong. He'll leave out a word or transpose a word.

I remember once talking to one of our big columnists years ago. He said to me, "You're a good friend of Jack Benny's. Why does he always look so unhappy?" This was when he was on top in radio.

And I said, "Maybe Jack's afraid to drop all the way down to second place."

He took out his pad and wrote: "He's afraid he'll drop down to second place."

I said, "You have to say *all the way* down to second place."

He said, "Why is that?"

I said, "Dropping down to second place may seem catastrophic, so unless you say *all the way* down you don't point out that it's not that bad."

He said, "Well, that's not for my column. I write a certain way and that's it."

To what extent did studying journalism in college help you develop the craft of comedy writing?

It had nothing to do with it. I was on the college paper. I ran a column called "The Dyspeptic" with short comedy lines. I wanted to write comedy all of the time. I was rather shy then, never spoke up, but I was able to do it on the typewriter. After a while it just comes to you.

Someone taking a course in creative writing or in how to write a novel can learn certain basic methods or techniques. Are there also rules for writing jokes?

Yes, when you are writing in conference, as a group. When we write, we hone it, we refine it to make it say what it's supposed to say. Somebody will suggest this word should be here. Everybody has his own idea of how a joke will get a laugh. The basic rule is that it should be phrased correctly. A word out of place will spoil the whole joke.

I suppose the "all the way down to second place" is a good example of that. Could you give another?

When Nixon was running against Humphrey, my wife said, "Let's vote for Humphrey; we can always vote for Nixon next time." Now that joke was told back to me by a friend. He said, "Let's vote for Humphrey; we can vote for Nixon next time." He thought he was being funny, but he left out the key word. You've got to say *always* to make it work. Otherwise it doesn't mean anything.

A great guy for this is Jack Benny. If you give him a joke he wants it phrased correctly. He called up once from Canada. He was coming into town during a newspaper strike here. We're very friendly. He said, "Have you got a good joke about the newspaper strike?"

I said, "Yes, I have one." Everybody was reading the *Christian Science Monitor* in New York at the time. So I gave him this joke: "I was reading the *Christian Science Monitor*. The news in that paper is just as terrible as it is in the other papers, only you *think* it's better."

Now that has to be told just like that. Of course, Jack did and it got a big laugh.

Is it important to know good grammar or be able to speak English well?

It's not important to making a joke come out. Will Rogers never used good grammar. He said, "The men who don't say 'ain't' ain't eating." But I think it gives the comedian more stature. You'll accept what they say. They don't sound like bums.

Unless they're being bums. Buddy Hackett wouldn't be expected to use good grammar. He's that type of guy. But when a fellow is an emcee of a show — nice-looking, immaculately dressed — he ought to use good speech. He doesn't have to use polysyllabics to prove he knows words, but at least he should use basic grammar. *He don't* is wrong.

One comedian the other night on television said something was "heart rendering." They should have rendered the fat out of his head first before they let him say that. One of the writers on the show should have told him that was the wrong thing to say.

For seventeen years you wrote "Easy Aces." What were the major differences in writing your own program compared to creating material for subsequent comedy shows?

Number one, we had no studio audience. We just did our stuff. We had a girl on the show named Marge who laughed every time Jane made a "malaprop" or I would say something under my breath. For instance, Jane would say, "I just went down to the ghetto to take a look at the Old Testament houses." Then I would mutter, "Holy Moses," or something to give the audience at home a chance to laugh. So it was easier writing. I just had to depend on what I thought was good for the characters.

Then the major difference in writing for your show and writing the later radio and TV shows was that the lines didn't have to be as strong.

Right. Lines like when Jane says, "I want to become an actress."

And I say, "Oh, not that story again."

And Jane says, "Yes, you will!"

I haven't said, "We're not going to hear that story again," but she's said, "Yes, you will." She's a

jump ahead. It's not a big joke, but it's in her character. And we don't give her any jokes that dissipate
her character. A lot of times, on the air, I've noticed
comics in a sketch do a joke that destroys the character because it gets a big laugh.

It's out of character.

Yes, and it destroys it, but they know it's a big
laugh and they leave it in. I would never do that with
Jane's character, nor would I ever do it with Como.
You write for whomever you write. You can't have
Perry Como in a big love scene saying something
that isn't in character. He's as careful about his
songs—you have to be careful when you are writing
for him.

**Say you were writing for Jackie Gleason as Ralph
Cramden in "The Honeymooners."**

You write exactly what fits the character. You
don't give him a joke about Einstein's theory of
relativity, because he wouldn't be supposed to know
about it. Even if you know it's a great joke, you save
it for somebody else. There is another difference
between writing humor and writing comedy. Humor
can read well. Dorothy Parker—she was one of our
great humor writers—we used her stuff on "The Big
Show" and it never got anything. The audience just
listened. Then Dorothy Parker wasn't allowed on the
radio anymore—that Red channels thing. One week,
all of a sudden, we were told the Dorothy Parker spot
was out, but they said we had to write a spot to
replace it. And Tallulah said, "You authors obviously couldn't write anything as good as Dorothy
Parker."

I said, "Of course not; we can't write that well,
but we'll write something that will probably play
better."

So we wrote a sketch about Tallulah getting on

the subway for the first time. It became Tallulah against conformity. When she discovered there was a subway she said, "Dahling, I found the most marvelous way to get across the city." She said to the conductor, "I want a private room." It really got big laughs.

You were playing against Tallulah's elegance, her being a very sophisticated lady.

That's right. When she tried to enter the subway, she said to the guard, "I'll have to give you a check for a dime." She did the sketch as a monologue.

What is the difference between writing a humorous column for the *Saturday Review* and writing jokes that can be delivered by a comedian?

The humorous pieces are just plain humor, but there are always some quotable jokes in them. "The State of the Theater Today" is a piece that tells how the theater all started with a girl with on a G-string. I mention this play in Greenwich Village in which everybody was arrested for nudity. I wrote, "Years ago in the Village, O'Neill, Schisgal, and Gilroy wrote plays that bared their souls. Nowadays they bare their actors." Jokes like that you can say. A comic can deliver. I try to get some of those in there!

Is writing an article the same as writing for radio— in that you're not pressured to come up with the so-called "big joke"? And it's being read!

Yes, it's being read, but some jokes can work both ways. "Baring their actors rather than their souls" can read well, and it could be funny if a comedian said it on stage. A comic could reword it. "It used to be an author bared his soul; now he bares his cast." That can get a laugh in a theater on a stage or in a nightclub. Some guy picked it up and put it in the paper the other day.

We also did "Easy Aces" with an audience later

on, a half-hour show, each show complete. So then
we wrote for an audience that was there. We had to
have laughs all the way along, and they were pretty
solid laughs.

Then the jokes had to be stronger?

They had to be strong jokes. Not obvious jokes.
But they were jokes that an audience who knew the
characters would laugh at. You can get big laughs
built on character. Jack Benny is the best example.
When he was appearing at the Fontainebleau Hotel
[Miami Beach] he said, "This is a beautiful hotel.
I've seen all the hotels in Las Vegas and I never
dreamed there would be a hotel like this. A place like
this must have cost forty or fifty thousand dollars."
He has all those years of character going for him to
back up that joke.

**In a *New York Times* article by Richard P. Hunt, you
were quoted as saying, "Audiences laugh in
rhythm. A good comedian can tell two jokes, say
nothing the third time, and still get a laugh because
they expect to laugh." Would you explain that?**

Well, Berle showed me he could do that once. He
did that in a warm-up. He said, "I'll show you how I
can get 'em to laugh and I'll say nothing the third
time." He pulled a fast joke *(laugh)* threw another
fast joke *(laugh)*. These were short jokes—one-
liners. Then he said double talk and they laughed
again.

Double talk?

Words that didn't make any sense.

But in the same rhythm as the other lines.

That's right. Now my friend Groucho, when I go
out on lecture tours I tell this story about him
because I was there when it happened. A priest
stopped him once in an elevator and said, "Mr. Marx,
I want to thank you for all the years of pleasure

you've given my mother on your television show. She would be very happy that I spoke to you."

And Groucho said, "I didn't know you fellas were allowed to have mothers." Which is a big joke, right?"

Now I heard him tell his own joke the other night on a television show and it came out like this: "I met this priest in an elevator, and he said, 'Groucho, I want to thank you for all the years of pleasure you've given *me* with your radio shows."

And Groucho said, "I didn't know you fellas were allowed to have mothers."

So I said to him afterwards, "You didn't tell that joke right." And I explained what he had done and he said, "Well, it got a big laugh there!"

I said, "They were laughing in rhythm—they laughed at your two jokes ahead of that. The minute you stopped they knew it was time to laugh, so they did."

That's another example of what you talked about earlier—about leaving out a word. I wonder how much of the laugh Groucho got can be attributed to his being an accepted comedy name.

Years ago he told me he made up a joke and put it in a play—I think it was *Coconuts*. He had great writers on that play—George Kaufman, Morrie Ryskind. He made up this joke and they tried to get him to take it out and he never would. Chico came out with a piece of ice and Groucho said, "How much do you want for the ice?"

He says, "Fifty cents!"

And Groucho says, "For fifty cents I could buy my own Eskimo and make my own ice." It never got anything.

Now it's years later. Groucho's been on "You Bet Your Life." They all know who he is. I was living

with him out on the Coast while working on a
picture, and he said, "C'mon, let's go into Beverly
Hills. I want to get a cake knife." So we walked into
this place and he said to the salesgirl, "How much
for this cake knife?"

She says, "A dollar and a quarter."

He says, "For a dollar and a quarter I could get
my own Eskimo and make my own cake knife." And
it got the biggest laugh you ever heard.

He did the same thing with a hat a little while
afterwards. He went in for a hat. Twenty-two dollars. "For twenty-two dollars I could get an Eskimo
and make my own hat." Got a big laugh. The rub is,
they know him; they recognize him. He has his own
moustache now—he doesn't paint one on. They
know him on the street, and they think he's funny;
that's all. He gets laughs; they don't figure out what
it is or why. People don't care.

**Then it's much more difficult for the unknown,
unrecognized comedian to get laughs.**

Yes, that's right. A lot of times you can bet on a
joke. I've stopped doing that. Tallulah was a baseball fan, so I had a joke where she says, "I feel
terrible about what they do to the umpires. The first
time they go out on the field the band strikes up 'Oh,
say, can you see.'"

And the producer, who didn't know baseball,
said, "That's not a very funny joke!"

And I said, "I'll bet you a dollar it gets a laugh!"
And it didn't get anything.

Now, years later, I did it on a show called "That
Was the Week That Was." I tied it up like this. There
was a strike of the National League umpires in
Chicago at the time, and I said, "They went on strike
protesting the band. Every time they came out on the
field the band played, 'Oh, say, can you see.'" It got a

big laugh from that audience—a very big laugh.

But it didn't get anything with Tallulah. They did other jokes on baseball with Tallulah that got big laughs. Obvious things like: "If you were on third base and there's two strikes on a batter and you're a run behind and it's starting to rain, how would you get home?" "You have to take a taxi!"

How do you explain the fact that the "say, can you see" joke didn't work for Tallulah?

I don't know. It's very possible that the umpires' being on strike made the subject more familiar to the audience. It was more topical. See, every humorist has to write for his times. The jokes we wrote fifteen years ago or even two years ago are gone, stale.

You write for your times. You know, all the television shows are timeless; they're out in space somewhere. The situation comedies: Lucy never gets a Mother's Day card, never gets a Christmas present. The shows are manufactured. They have nothing to do with the American scene today. I think that's a waste of time.

In a *New York Times* story by John P. Shanley, you said, "The Perry Como Program required a gentle kind of comedy—the hardest to write." What is "gentle comedy?"

Gentle is not insult. You can insult people very easily. Perry won't insult anybody. He never would say, "You've got the mind of a two-year-old and I think you ought to give it back to him." Those are the easiest kinds of jokes to write.

We did do insult jokes on "The Big Show" with Tallulah on radio. George Sanders was on the show quite a bit. We found out that he did short bursts best—lines like "Indeed!"

Tallulah would say to him, "I have no patience

with actors who won't leave the stage when their time is up. I hope and pray that I'll be able to make my exit gracefully and graciously."

He says, "And did you?" It's an insult joke even though it's gentle. Perry wouldn't do that joke. It goes against his character. Perry is a nice, quiet guy.

Why is gentle comedy the hardest to write?

It's easy to think up nasty things. It's just like writing a bad review for the theater, a play on Broadway. It's easy to get quotes. You remember quotes of theatrical critics only when they pan the play. After he went to see *Hamlet* the critic wrote: "Who wrote *Hamlet*, Shakespeare or Sir Francis Bacon? After last night's performance, you dig up their graves and the one who turned over is the one who wrote it." He's turned a phrase and made a caustic comment so people quote it. Gentle comedy is hard to write.

Was the "Easy Aces" comedy considered gentle?

That was gentle comedy, although I said a lot of things that had bite to them. Jane says she wants to go on the stage and become rich and famous, and then, she says, "I'll divorce you!"

I say, "Promises! Promises!"

She says, "No, not in musical comedy. I don't want that." Then she says, "Although my friends do say I sing like an angel."

I say, "Like an angel? Can't you wait till you get there?" That's insult comedy, but the edge isn't as sharp.

Generally speaking, why is comedy more difficult to write than straight dialogue?

It isn't for me. Straight dialogue is more difficult for me to write. It's torture. I can write it, but I just have no interest in it. I'd rather write a comedy line, or, if I write straight dialogue, I try to turn a phrase. Like I once wrote a thing: *You can't overestimate the unimportance of practically everything.* I enjoy turning a phrase around to make it say something besides the obvious.

Is the ability to write comedy a craft anyone can learn, or are you born with it?

You have to have something to go with it. There are some guys that never, never will be any good. And there are guys who can do it. But it's something that you learn. You can get better at it the longer you do it.

Do you think funnier today than you did when you first started?

I write better today than I did before, because shows now have something to write for. When I was first writing for television all you had to write was: "And now we take you to Latin America where you hear the rhythm of Perez Prado's orchestra." Sometimes the guests on the variety shows literally had nothing to say. An actress comes to New York. She's just finished singing three hundred songs, and now she's going to do a duet with the host. There's nothing to discuss with her.

You try to get a little comedy into it here and there, if you can. When we had guests for Tallulah, it took us an hour sometimes to find a talking point. Once you got a target you probably could write on something.

Very often a critic or reviewer will say, "He's a natural comedian." Is there such a thing as a natural comedy writer?

I don't know. Sometimes. I guess there are. Once there was a guy who wanted to come in and write with me. A very wealthy guy, and he was very funny. A friend of mine was here, and he said, "I don't know why he wouldn't be a good writer. His insurance is paid up, he has no mortgages to worry about, his car is paid for. He's so wealthy he should be relaxed, be able to think."

So I said to my friend, "But if you put him in a room with a typewriter and said, 'I want you to write this particular spot about this particular subject, and don't come out until it's written,' the typewriter would come out first." This wealthy guy could ad-lib something funny during a conversation. But for someone to sit down and *write* funny is something else. A guy once asked Berle if I was a good writer, and he said, "He writes funny letters!"

What is the difference then between the man who can say funny things and the man who is able to sit down at the typewriter and write to order?

Well, the wealthy guy could probably do it at the typewriter if he picks his own subject and he's got something to say about it, but it's got to be something he can do, something that's peculiar to him. But if he's got to pick a subject that Perry Como's going to talk about or Garry Moore or one of those actors, he's in trouble.

Is it a question of discipline or training?

It takes time. When I first went to work for Perry nobody told me what his peculiarities were, what his taboos were. I was just stabbing until we had talks and talks and I found out. I used to cajole him into doing jokes.

We went to St. Louis once to do a show, and Perry wanted a little monologue. A monologue for Perry was three good jokes right at the start. So on the plane going out I thought of a good joke. A month before we did our show from Rome in Italy, the

Vatican, a Christmas show. So the joke was: "Last month we were at the Vatican, this week in St. Louis. It's always nice to have the Cardinals with us!" And he argued with me that the joke wouldn't get a laugh, but he finally agreed to do it. It not only got a laugh; it got applause.

But the point I'm trying to make is, now that I won that argument you'd think I was set for next week. No; it was the same thing all over again. I had him do a line the first show back after the summer: "I was trapped in my house all summer with my kids playing the jukebox, records, and all that. It's been the summer of my discotheque!"

Now I saw his eyes go up on that joke, and when we finished reading the script he said, "I don't know about that joke. Let's give it to Frank Gallop [*Como's announcer*]. But I ought to have an answer for him."

So I gave Perry the easiest one. Gallop says, "This has been the summer of your discotheque."

And Perry says, "This'll be the winter of your replacement."

When we finally did the joke, it got a big laugh at rehearsal and at dress rehearsal with a studio audience. Later, laughingly, Perry said, "If I'd known it would get that big a laugh I wouldn't have given it to Frank."

I said, "Let's take it away from him."

He said, "Oh, no. You can't do that." That's the kind of gentleman Perry was.

As you look back now, was there anything in your background or environment that you believe motivated you to go into comedy?

No, except when I was about nine or ten, I remember I loved cartoons. Then later I used to love

reading humor. In those days it was magazines like
Judge, Life—those magazines had comedy in them.
**Can you explain why you were interested in the
cartoons and jokes?**

They were just childish whims. Then later I
thought it was smart to say something chic and
clever. As I mentioned before, I wrote a column in
college called "The Dyspeptic." It was a guy who
suffered from dyspepsia and made sarcastic
remarks about everything.

**Do you subscribe to the theory that there are only
seven original jokes?**

No; I don't know what they are. I don't even know
what that means. There are no original jokes if you
want the truth of it. Fred Allen once got me a book
called *Toastmasters Handbook*—two volumes. He
said, "You see that book?"

I said, "Yes." We were in front of this bookstore.

He said, "You oughta get it."

I said, "You don't use joke books, do you?"

He said, "Sometimes they'll lead you to a twist
on a joke." So he bought me those two books and I
never used them.

Once I was writing some jokes about a mother-
in-law. Jane's mother was coming to visit us, and I
needed some one-liners. So I looked through the
book, and the first joke I saw in there was a joke I
thought I had made up. And this book was a hundred
years old. So I just go on the theory that somewhere,
somebody must've thought of it before. I did a
phrase yesterday—I said, "You can accomplish this
magic by a simple sleight of mind." Now nobody's
ever said "sleight of mind," as far as I know. To a
comedian that may not be a big boff. But I'd rather
write that than a big joke.

What is the function of the head writer?

He decides which jokes should go into the script for the show and he alienates the writers from him. When they turn in their assignments, the head writer says, "Yes, that's pretty good," and he puts it over on the other side of his desk, like he's going to use it later. Then he turns off for the rest of the day and sulks. Most of the guys don't care. When Jay Burton worked for me, he didn't care if you used his joke or not. He figured I'd use it someplace sooner or later.

Do you have the writers write their assignments at home?

No. We'd work right here in the office. We'd start with page one. They don't go home and write and then bring in stuff. We'd work on the script and the jokes together. I'd say, "Now this is the way I want the script to go."

We had Rudy Vallee on the show once. He wrote us a three-page letter saying he wanted to be known as the star of *How to Succeed in Business without Really Trying,* and he didn't want to mention "The Wiffenpoof Song," the megaphone, the Connecticut Yankee days and all that. Then he had a page of stuff he *wanted* to do. And it was pretty bad.

So Perry says, "What do we do about it?"

I said, "I think you oughta cancel him!"

He said, "I can't do that!"

So at our script meeting I said to the guys, "Let's write the script the way we want. I think if we do one joke that he gets a big laugh with he won't mind it."

The first joke was—Perry says, "Rudy, I'm glad you could make our show, because you've always been one of my favorites. Your career has been, eh, has been, eh . . ."

And Rudy says, "I wish you'd stop saying *has*

been!" At rehearsal he got a big laugh with it, and everything was all right.

So the head writer—

Is supposed to start things off. We had Bob Crosby on the show once. This was some years ago on "The Milton Berle Show." I said, "Let's do a script for Bob Crosby without mentioning Bing." Because the guy made it on his own.

So I had Bob call Milton on the phone—a split screen—and he says, "Milton, this is Bob Crosby."

Milton says, "Hello, Bob. How's everything in Hollywood?"

And Bob says, "He's fine!"

Then his main function is to coordinate—

And say, "This is the pattern, this is what the spot should be." Sometimes it takes an hour to figure out what the subject's going to be, and sometimes it's a lot of wasted effort.

For instance, that Crosby joke. Berle came to me after rehearsal and said, "Shouldn't that be *'Bing* is fine' instead of *'He's* fine'?"

And I said, "No."

He said, "You *mean* Bing, don't you?"

I said, "I think it's classier to do it this way."

Then Bob Crosby called, "Shouldn't it be 'Bing'? That's my first joke, and I'd like to make sure I get a big laugh."

I answered, "Bob, that's what we're trying to do. You should get the laugh."

He said, "Well, I'd feel more comfortable if—"

I said, "Tell you what. If 'He's fine' doesn't get a laugh, you say, 'And how's *your* brother?' to Milton."

Crosby said, "That's great!"

He got on the air; he said, "He's fine!" They laughed; they applauded.

Then Bob says, "And how's *your* brother?" He said it anyhow.

In that *Times* article by Richard Hunt, you explained the ingredients of a successful comedy show. You said there "has to be a partnership—a marriage between the writer and the performer." What specific problems does a writer have to contend with? Temperament? Judgment?

Well, with each performer it's different. Perry will not do political jokes. In fact, everything we wrote was suspect. We once went to Canada to do a show about the Expo. I didn't know what to write about Canada, but I found a good joke in the *World Almanac*—that's an awful place to find a joke. I found: "Russia is first in the world in area and Canada is second," and I added: "I guess you thought it was Avis!" So right away the juxtaposition of Canada and Avis meant something terrible. And I argued and had to swear on *Variety* we never meant anything by it.

Perry had no temperament. He's one of the nicest gentlemen I've ever worked for. The only thing is, there were certain things he wouldn't do or say, things he didn't feel were right to say. With Berle, we respected each other from a distance. I think Berle is one of the greatest nightclub comedians there is. He knows how to handle an audience, but he wouldn't do a lot of things we wanted to do. I kind of insisted. At the point I started to work for him he had dropped way down in the ratings. I took the job only because I thought it might be a challenge. I knew I was going to have trouble with him.

But I learned a lot from Berle. I didn't know what "laughy" was. He said, "You've gotta make a joke laughy." I didn't want to let him know I didn't know what "laughy" was; he was paying me a lot of money. So I took one of the writers aside and asked him. He said, "It means a joke that can make all of the audience laugh at the same time!" I told Berle that sometimes you didn't have to do that.

Perhaps Berle's insistence on having "laughy" jokes was a holdover from his vaudeville background when the audiences weren't as sophisticated and he had to really lay out the joke.

That's a good point, and maybe that's where it started. He knew how a joke would go in a nightclub, but—Once we had a joke in the show about the little girl, Max. It was a show about politics. He says, "She's so dumb she thinks Washington, D.C., stands for Denver, Colorado." That was the joke.

So he called me into his office, locked the door, before a big day's rehearsal on a Tuesday morning. He says, "You know that joke about D.C. I've been rehearsing this since Thursday [this is Tuesday]. I just got the joke."

So I said, "Congratulations!" I didn't know what to say.

He said, "No, I mean it. If I didn't get it, the people won't get it."

So I said, "I think they will."

He said, "No, no. It needs a joke in here like. . ." He always said that—"it needs a joke like . . ." "She thinks the secretary of the interior is a doctor that studies X-rays."

I said, "That's a great joke; put it in there!"

He said, "No, that's an old joke!"

I said, "I never heard it before!"

He said, "You'll think of something."

Now I figure he's got a whole day where he directs, conducts the orchestra, handles the scenery, the costumes. He's busy all day; he'll never think about it. I come back around three o'clock. He says, "Did you think of a joke?"

I said, "Yes. 'She's so dumb she thinks the electoral college is a school for television repairman.'"

He said, "Electrical?"

I said, "No, Milton; that's no good. I'll think of something else!"

Now the show is running late with rehearsal, and I'm just about to go home. I didn't have to stay and watch rehearsal; it wasn't in my contract. He says, "Did you think of a joke?" Now I know there are certain words Milton likes, like "necking."

I said, "She's so dumb she thinks the Democratic Party is a party where the girls let the fellas neck."

He said, "That's great!"

I said, "Have it put on the cue cards, Milton!"

He said, "I'll remember *that!*"

I said, "Tell the fella; he'll put it on there."

He said, "No. I'll remember!"

Now I go home and I watch the show and he says, "She's so dumb she thinks the Republican Party is— I mean, she said, the Democratic Party— Well, I loused that up." There went a whole day's work.

"I loused that up " got a bigger laugh than the necking joke would have gotten!

What is required to have a good working relationship with a comedian?

I don't know. I used to worry about that years ago, but I don't let it knock me out as much now. You just have to go along with him on some things, and you try to get your points across on others. Sid Caesar, who I think is probably the greatest sketch actor around, is bad at monologues. But he knows what he wants. When I went to work for him we had some very friendly talks in advance. I went away, and I wrote the script.

I came to him with the first show and he says, "You wrote it?"

I said, "Yeah."

He said, "Gee, I wanted to sit with you while you wrote it!"

I said, "We can't do that. You'll be sitting there thinking about what you're gonna say while I'm thinking about all the other characters, too!"

Well, they called in the lawyers and the managers, and finally they decided we could write it in advance, but Sid reserved the right to break it open and do whatever he wanted to do. He usually put in a lot of *shtiklech*.*

He liked to do the kind of sketch he called "walkie-talkie." He didn't like to sit at a desk or talk to a guy sitting at one—he had to have action. He's great at that. I learned a lot from him. But I still got him to do a sketch in which he just sat there. It was the funniest sketch I ever wrote.

But in answer to your question . . . you go along. You compromise. You say, "Let's try this, see if it works." Some comics don't know. They take anybody's word but the writer's. That's why writers are held in such low esteem.

In a *Cosmopolitan* interview with Maurice Zolotow you said, "Actors are selfish, egocentric, emotionally immature" and that "many of them are incapable of being sincere." Did you mean comedians specifically or performers in general?

Well, I've tempered that a lot. Most people are all

---

*A Jewish word meaning "little pieces."

right. I just go along with what they do. Some people think *I'm* egocentric and inconsiderate and immature. But I try not to be, and I want them to try not to be. I don't argue about that.

The thing that's frustrating is when an actor doesn't trust your judgment. I went to a rehearsal of a show I did for television, "The Big Party," with Alan King, Zsa Zsa Gabor, Deborah Kerr, and some other glamor gal. They had a little bit where they talked about their dresses. One says. "Mine is a Balenciaga." One says, "Mine is a Dior." And the other one says so-and-so. And they're arguing over which one is more beautiful. Finally, one says, "Let's get a man's opinion about it—Alan!" And they call him over and they say, "We'd like to have a man's opinion about our clothes."

And Alan says, "Will I do until one comes along?" But that line wasn't in the script.

Afterwards I went to Alan and said, "Why do you say 'Will I do until one comes along?'"

He said, "Well, I oughta have something there."

I said, "Do you want people to think you're a homosexual?"

He said, "I thought it was funny, and Abe Burrows, the director, thought it was, too."

I said, "I don't think that's the right thing to say."

He said, "Well, I need some joke there."

I said, "Maybe if we change the straight line we can get a joke."

He said, "OK. Where are the other writers?"

I said, "I think this is a one-man job. I can go away to Maine for two weeks and take a shot at it, or maybe I can go into the next room."

So I changed the straight line to: "Alan, have

you ever given a thought to women's clothes?"
And Alan was to say, "Oh, off and on . . . I mean,
now and then!" That was the joke. And I gave it to
him. A half-hour later I see him talking to his agent
and he says, "OK!" His agent said it was OK. That
was a kind of let-down for me. That's typical of
actors—they're not certain.

Are there exceptions?

Well, Bob Hope will never argue about a joke.
He'll come over and say, "Are you in love with that
joke?"

I'll say, "No, I'm not in love with it. Why don't
you try it. If it doesn't get anything we'll give you
something else."

Now he does it at rehearsal with the orchestra,
and it gets a big laugh. But he's that kind of guy. He
tries to be accommodating. Of course, he also brings
his writers with him.

I remember one time, at a rehearsal of "The Big
Show" with Tallulah—we worked on that show
seven days a week and three nights—Perry Como
was a guest. He finished singing, and Bob Hope was
next. Hope says, "That Perry Como—he's got a voice
like the mating call of a mashed potato." Then he
says to me, "What the hell does that mean?"

I said, "I don't know—I'll tell them to take it out."
He says, "No, don't bother."

I said, "Why not? You like all the other jokes. It's
the only change you've made."
He said, "No, I'll try it."

I said, "That's not even a joke—it won't get
anything!"

But he did it on the air, and it got one of the
biggest laughs on the show that night. That's Bob
Hope.

Do most comedians have a good idea of what is funny and what material will work for them?

I think they know what works best for *them*, how they should say it, and whether it's in their character. They have some image of themselves. They make mistakes sometimes. If I were working for Bob Hope, I wouldn't give him a Groucho Marx line.

In that *Times* article you talked about the Sid Caesar show, and you pointed out that Sid played so many roles that he didn't have an image. You said—

I didn't mean he didn't have an image with the audience. I meant he himself didn't know who *he* was. Danny Kaye could be very funny as a German or an Italian, as Sid could be, but Sid as himself, coming out in front of an audience and telling a few jokes—he was uncomfortable. So I never bothered with that.

You also said, "Danny Kaye had the same problem but he developed an image of himself and now he plays that image like a part." How can a writer help a comedian find an image?

They usually have some idea. You can't help Sid Caesar because he's just not a monologist and he's given up trying to be. Danny Kaye is a great monologist. He has a great personality. He has great rapport with the audience. Sid wants to be liked, but he doesn't endear himself until he becomes the person he is playing. He can do any character.

According to a newspaper article in the *New York Telegram* some years ago, there are probably fewer than two hundred comedy writers. If there is such a great need for laughter, why are there so few people to provide it?

Because nobody can get into television. I get letters from people every day who want to become comedy writers. I tell them: "The only way you can become a comedy writer is to have a credit. And the only way you can get a credit is to write for television." They won't take you. They'd rather have a comedy writer out there they can handle. They can't tell him, "We don't want any innovations!" They want the same kind of stuff all the time. It's run off— Xeroxed every day. They don't try new ones. I've broken in a lot of new writers.

For instance?

Billy Angeles and Buzz Corham, who have written for Carol Burnett. Frank Peppiatt and Johnny Allsworth—they started here. They had a good comedy sense. Jay Burton is the best one I ever had. He's great.

In an article you wrote for the *Saturday Review,* **"Writer Is a Dirty Word," you implied that "the comedy writer's integrity and importance have been consistently minimized by the comedians, the industry, and the public." Since the writer is an integral part of the entertainment creativity, why does this climate exist?**

Because most actors won't admit they have writers. They think they've made up all this stuff or begin to think it. When George Sanders came on "The Big Show" he was getting big laughs with what we wrote for him. We found out that two- or three-word answers got a big laugh for him. We had a straight line once: Tallulah says to him, "George, I envy you. You're so good at everything. You're not only an actor; you've been in films, on the stage. You're a pianist, an organist; you compose music; you've just invented a gadget for the navy; you design lamps. How do you do all these things?" And that's as far as we got.

We sat for about forty-five minutes thinking of a

one-line answer, and we couldn't think of one. Mr. Sanders happened to come into town early and he dropped into the office and said, "Hello, gentlemen."

I said, "Come in, George. Here's the straight line, and you tell us the answer."

So he looked at it. He sat there for about five minutes, and he was getting red in the face. Then he said, "You want me to say a line here."

I said, "Yes. You can't say 'Indeed' or anything like that."

So finally he said, "Well, I'm sure you gentlemen will think of something!" And he walked out.

We didn't think of anything, so I said, "Let's let it go. We'll finish the script. Maybe it'll come to us."

That night at home I put it in the typewriter, and suddenly I got it. I didn't take any credit for it because I should have thought of it earlier. So the next day I handed the script to George, and I said, "By the way, we thought of that line. When she says to you, 'How do you do all these things?' you say, 'Magnificently!'"

He thought for a moment, then he said, "Naturally!" He began to feel that would be the natural thing for him to say. But why couldn't he have thought of it?

In that same article, you wrote, "Television will have reached its maturity when it realizes, as have the stage and movies, that successful entertainment depends not alone on the stars who play it but the stars in combination with those who write the words the stars speak." Has television reached its maturity?

I don't think so. Actors are still antagonistic toward writers. At least most of them. I imagine Carol Burnett listens to her writers. I think Dean

Martin does what his writers tell him to. But there are a lot of them who are constantly fighting. Like the comedian who once said to me, "Who are you writing against this year?" That's the attitude of these guys. They don't like to think anybody writes for them. No, I don't think the situation has changed much.

Mel
BROOKS

Mel Brooks was born Melvin Kaminsky on June 28, 1926, in Brooklyn, New York. After working briefly as a stand-up comic in the Catskills, he wrote "Your Show of Shows" for ten years. Following that, he created an Academy Award-winning short, *The Critic* (1963).

Brooks then teamed with Carl Reiner for *The 2000-Year-Old Man* comedy album and later joined Dick Cavett on some classic Ballantine Beer TV commercials. His next partner, in creating the "Get Smart" television series, was Buck Henry, scenarist for *The Graduate,* which starred Anne Bancroft. (The actress married Mel Brooks in 1964.)

In the past few years, Mel Brooks has concentrated on directing the screenplays he has written. First was *The Producers* (1967), starring Zero Mostel and Gene Wilder. Brooks's next triumph was *The Twelve Chairs* (1971), for which he wrote the musical theme, directed, and also played a starring role.

Then came *Blazing Saddles,* voted funniest motion picture of 1974 by the American Academy of

Humor. After that came another record with Carl Reiner—*The 2000-Year-Old Man Is Now 2000 and Thirteen.*

His film *Young Frankenstein,* which he wrote with Gene Wilder, premiered in 1975. He also co-created the television sitcom "When Things Were Rotten."

This talk took place in Mel Brooks's office at the Burbank Studios of Warner Brothers. He had spent much of the day editing film, and despite apparent fatigue rallied to the questions with vigor and enthusiasm.

His "work" clothes are a blue short-sleeved shirt, khaki Levis, black socks, and brown loafers. Referred to in *Playboy* magazine as the "American Rabelais" and "unarguably a comic genius," Brooks smiles often, displaying a set of almost perfectly formed teeth.

There is a suggestion of weariness in the tanned features, but the alert expression signals—as *Time* magazine put it—"someone deeply dedicated to the perpetration of mindlessness over matter."

Mel Brooks is of the "self-educated" school of writers. He surprised the interviewer with an amazingly broad vocabulary and a perceptive, literate mind.

Unquestionably, Brooks is a giant contributor to the world of comedy, brilliantly lampooning society's flaws and follies. When showing his serious side during this discussion, he projected a gentleness and warmth that demonstrate great sensitivity.

Paul Gauguin quit his job as a bank clerk and

became a great painter. Woodrow Wilson was a college professor before he entered politics and became president. Did you have another profession before you became a comedy writer?

I was an actor in summer stock. I played ingenue roles, and I was very good, except one day I was forced to dress with the other girls. They didn't have enough dressing rooms, and I was found out. Only because of the way I used the john. The way I flushed, certain incredible sounds gave me away. Otherwise they never would have known. Because I really took care that nobody should see. Now, what was the question?

Did you have another profession before you became a comedy writer?

I didn't have a *profession*. I *still* don't have a profession. A profession to a Jew is a doctor or a lawyer or maybe an Indian chief. No, I had many jobs, *little* jobs.

Did you always want to be a comedy writer?

Not really. That's curious. I'm directing now to protect myself as a writer, and I became a comedy writer out of self-defense, to protect myself as a comedian to make sure the material was OK. Know what I mean?

Not exactly.

I started in the Catskill Mountains. I was a drummer in a little five-piece band. The comic got sick and I took over for him, and I made a hit, but I was stuck with: "Good evening, ladies and germs. Welcome to a bang-up variety show. I just flew in from Chicago and boy are my arms tired."

"I met a girl in Chicago. You wanna hear how skinny? She was so skinny I took her to a restaurant. The waiter said, 'Check your umbrella?'"

"In that hotel I got into a room that was so small the doorknob got into bed with you. The mice were hunchback."

All that junk. And I was fed up with that. The boss liked me and wanted me to be the comic. So what I did was this, I was looking for material when I said to myself, "Why am I looking for jokes when life literally abounds in comedy if you just look around you?"

The day before I did a show, the maid was locked in the linen closet. And she was pounding on the door and screaming in Yiddish: "Luz mir aroise! Luz mir aroise!" Let me out! Let me out! So that night my opening line, I said, "Good evening, ladies and gentlemen. Luz mir aroise!" The place fell down. I realized that all one really had to do was just observe. Observe and slightly exaggerate, and you had comedy. Instead of creating a mythical premise for a stupid joke, I found playing off truth got the best results.

In discussing their craft, comedy writers usually talk about cadence, rhythm, formula jokes—the basic tools of the profession—

Tools are not to be put down because they are technical measures; they are supportive devices in comedy. There are also phonetic values in certain words that will insure a laugh. But tools have very little to do with the essential talent or genius.

That is the after-effect?

Yeah. That's part of the *craft* of comedy. Instead of saying "salmon," "turkey" is a funnier sound. It just helps. In writing the Sid Caesar show all those years, we naturally went to the letter *k. Chicken, turkey* . . .

Was Sid Caesar the first comedian you wrote for after you decided to write for yourself?

Sid had been working up in the Catskills also as a comedian and a saxophone player. I got to know him slightly through a mutual friend, Don Appel, who worked with Sid at the Avon Lodge. When Sid played the Roxy Theatre [New York], I went and renewed my acquaintance with him.

This was a couple of years later?

Yeah. We were just friendly, and then he told me about this thing called television. Like radio with pictures. It was a scary thing. Nobody knew anything about it. This was in 1947. In 1948 Sid was in the "Admiral Broadway Review," and he asked me to drop by and punch up a few things for him. I wasn't a comedy writer then. He just knew me as a comic. As a matter of fact, I was interested in directing. I was directing a little play in Red Bank, New Jersey. And I took some time out, and I worked with Sid for fifty bucks a week on this "Admiral Broadway Review," just to pick up a little extra bread.

What did Sid mean when he said "punch up a few things"?

Max Liebman created a segment of the show called "Nonentities in the News." Sid played the part of the Jungle Boy, a man who comes out of the jungle. What I did was add a few jokes, like, "What's your greatest enemy?" and he said, "Buick! Only way to kill Buick, punch in grill! Hard! Buick die!"

That's how I began. Mel Tolkin was one of the regular writers. I was just the kid in the hall. I never got in the conference rooms. I waited outside for Sid to come out; then I'd follow him up the hall and throw him a few jokes.

Did Caesar's characters come from these early shows?

Yeah. Soon afterward came the German Professor. And I began specializing in that one for a while. Then we got into foreign movies. That was another good area for me to help with. Then slowly but surely I became recognized as a living, human person there, and I was validated the following season on "Your Show of Shows." On the second season of the show Max Liebman gave me credit. The credit was "Additional dialogue by"!

During this period did you still try to get jobs as a comedian?

I was working. I was doing little club dates as a comic during that period. And also doing dates as a drummer. Also selling blouses and dresses for Abilene Blouse and Dress Company.

Then giving jokes to Sid was an extra job?

Yeah. Then eventually it became a full-time job. I was employed as a comedy writer with credit, and it took up eighteen hours a day. And I was well compensated for it in those days.

Did this early work for Caesar help in your development?

Of course. Of course. Of course. Sid was, and still is, an amazing vehicle for a comedy writer's passion. He can do anything. Most comics were mimicking Bogart and Cagney. But Sid Caesar was mimicking people—human beings—in life. And he could do anything. From a one hundred percent American who would arrest a child sneaking onto a merry-go-round to an Italian farmer whose horse had died. He took off the horseshoes and ate beans at the same time. Sid widened the possibilities of comedy.

His comedic scope provided you with a broader opportunity to create.

Right. Had I worked for Berle or Hope early on, I could never have expanded so rapidly, in so many directions.

Why is that?

Because they simply didn't have the comic depth of Sid Caesar. With Sid our choices were infinite.

Berle and Hope did mostly jokes and sketches.

Yeah. Berle did a little more character work than Hope. Hope was always current, usually political, and relies a great deal on rhythm and wit. But Sid was at the opposite spectrum. He relied on pure characterization and played his characters very earnestly, never really asking for the laugh.

The laugh came out of the character, out of the situation.

Right. He always played it very seriously.

Was there a large writing staff?

For the first five years the comedy was written by Tolkin, myself, Lucille Kallen—a very talented lady—and of course Sid and Max Liebman and Carl Reiner and Howie Morris. Carl really made a major contribution. Then we hired Aaron Rubin; Phil Sharp; Joe Stein, who later did *Fiddler on the Roof;* Mike Stewart, who later did *Carnival* and *Hello Dolly;* and Danny and Doc Simon. Later, Woody Allen replaced Mike Stewart.

Then just as Hope's staff of writers learned their craft with him and went on to other assignments, "Your Show of Shows" provided an opportunity to—

We were like a Petri dish. That's a little dish where you grow colonies of germs, microbes, et cetera. The "Show of Shows" was like a Petri dish. You threw a comedy writer into it, and he just grew and mushroomed and then became twice his size. You learned so much in such a short time.

Part of the development was just rubbing elbows with the more experienced writers.

Not only as a comedy writer, but as a person. Mel Tolkin helped me in my first nervous breakdown. Actually, I was going bananas, and he was instrumental in my finding an analyst and teaching me there was such a thing called psychoanalysis.

But you did absorb a great deal of know-how from just working with these men.

Yes. But in all modesty I must say it was give and take, because I gave as much as I got. Now a really great thing happened on the "Show of Shows" that has been axiomatic for me in terms of my behavior as a comedy writer and a director, and that is, whatever is funny is *in*. Before that, in my comedy experience with other people, if I did a joke, they'd laugh but then they'd say, "No, we can't do that! That's in questionable taste." Or, "The audience won't get it."

But on the "Show of Shows" whatever made *us* laugh was the only test of what would go into the hopper. I feel that the audience is always ready to absorb anything you have in your mind. They don't reject it based on their own sense of values.

The *2000-Year-Old Man* **was the next major step in your career. How did that come about?**

Emotionally or psychologically that came out of pent-up feelings. Need. A great need for me to entertain. I never did join Carl, Howie, Sid, and Imogene Coca on the air. I was always with them, like a fight manager in the corner. I would just perform at parties after the show. Like the show jester. And Carl recognized that performing talent in me. Carl also had a sense of the comic importance of what we were saying.

Did you work from a script? Was anything down on paper?

Never. We did it into a tape recorder. I never knew who the characters would be except the 2000-year-old man. We did it at the recording studio just the way we did it at parties. Carl said, "I'll interview you as a 2000-year-old man. I'll make up some characters, and you'll simply respond." And it worked. Because it's the pressure that somehow helps catalyze comedy—the insanity.

But if someone writes for a show, he has to come in with something down on paper. He's had to write—

If on paper you were to write the things down that we said, they might not be so funny. The most important aspect of it was the *vocal* comedy, the *verbal* comedy. There's something in the voice, the excitement, the fighting for your life when Carl traps you. He chases me like I'm a mouse.

Has everything you've done since been off the top of your head or done under pressure?

No. No. You design specifically for the medium. For records, the best way for me and Carl to do was to just ad-lib it. A movie takes me eighteen months to write, because pieces have to be fashioned together and they have to work smoothly, and you need a good, strong clothesline to hang your comedy wash on. One method of work does not necessarily apply to anything but one specific medium.

What was the difference between the methods used in writing for Caesar and coming up with the situation comedy "Get Smart"?

If I wrote "Get Smart" the way I was writing for

Sid it would have been just a sketch. What I needed for a half-hour TV series was a condensation of the comedy in story form, not in sketch form. Sketch characters are there for just a moment. Series characters have to be more durable. So it was a completely different method. Buck Henry and I took about four months to write that pilot, and that was a half-hour. It was about twenty-four minutes of comedy. The "Show of Shows" was an hour and a half a week and took only four or five days. That's all the time we had to write it because they needed some time to rehearse it.

During the creating of "Get Smart" with Buck Henry, did the two of you stand up and rap the way you did with Carl Reiner?

Oh, yes. I love acting, so I acted out a lot of the parts and so did Buck. We played it together. By trial and error we found what worked best.

You did *The Producers* on your own. What's the difference between collaborating with the other two gentlemen and writing alone for motion pictures?

You're more unsure writing alone, because there's no immediate laughter. If you describe something in a room with five other comedy writers and you get an immediate, insane response—a big scream—then you know you're home with the joke. When you're sitting with just a secretary you can't go by what she laughs at. If you're sitting alone with a yellow pad and pencil, you can only hear yourself break up. But if near the end of the writing you can still laugh, you leave the joke in.

What about the screenplay form, the techniques?

Again it was trial and error. You remember I also directed that film.

Yes, but let's stick to the writing for the moment.

I read many screenplays. They were no help because each one was completely different. Some would give incredible physical directions to the actor and then instructions to the director. Some had none at all. Some wouldn't even have shots listed. What I did was simply make up cards. Each card was a scene. It's not new; everybody does that. We used to do that on the "Show of Shows."

Could you describe the process step by step?

Well, I took that little white card—for *The Producers*—and I wrote on it: "Scene One: Bialostak and the Old Ladies." Then I'd write that scene.

Before that didn't you have a treatment, a story line?

Yeah. First I had an outline. As a matter of fact, I was going to do it as a novel. Then it talked so much I thought it might be a play. Then it talked so much in so many different scenes I knew it was a film. It's as simple as that.

You started with an outline. Then you broke down the outline into scenes on the little cards?

Yeah.

And you wrote each scene from the card.

Yeah.

Then?

Then I kept throwing the cards out, changing cards.

Till you got what you felt was a working script?

Till I got a rough script I thought was pretty good. And I was still too much of a playwright. I had too much dialogue for a movie. Much too much minute characterization. And I had to replace the cards with visuals.

Is that something you again learned by trial and error?

Yeah. Just rereading it and getting pictures in

my head and seeing this way of doing it would take too long in a movie house. See, we're all movie directors in a sense, because we've gone to the movies all our lives. We all have a built-in, kind of unconscious movie rhythm from watching movies. We know instinctively when a scene is too long, when nothing visual is happening.

While you were filming *The Producers,* **what percentage of laughter was added to the finished product as a result of the actors?**

Much. Talk about ad-lib. In the end after you get a very good, fine, polished script and say, "I'm going to go with this," you add the actors' chemistry. You never know what's going to happen from moment to moment while you're filming. That's why I decided I would not have this movie done if I didn't direct. The actors made a tremendous contribution. It would not have been *The Producers* without Zero Mostel and Gene Wilder, in spite of a terrific script and my being in the director's seat— and Kenny Marx, who was brilliant as the German.

What advantage is there for the screenwriter to direct his own script?

It's invaluable. Every moment is like a little tile, and only the director-writer has the mosaic in his head and knows where every tile goes in order to make it work—for balance, for color.

Very often the author of a funny screenplay must turn it over to a director who doesn't have the comedic insight or background that you have.

When that happens the screenwriter should go into a dark place and cry for three and a half hours and wipe his tears and come out laughing into the sunlight once again. Or if he has any brains, has a little bit of general in him, he will protect his screen-

play by directing it. Or he'll take the money and run
and won't give a damn about what happens to it.

**In an interview with columnist Joyce Haber you
said, "Writers are sour and selfish and grudging.
Writers are very private, not collaborative people.
They have friends, but they're all in their own head.
Their friends are their characters. They're a little
nuts." Is that analysis intended for all writers or just
those who write comedy?**

No. I was talking about writers who wrote
longer works and lived with them. Not comedy
writers all bunched up in a room writing the "Show
of Shows." I was talking about novelists and people
who write screenplays, those who live with these
fantastic creatures.

**E. B. White once said, "Humor can be dissected as a
frog can, but the thing dies in the process and the
innards are discouraging to any but the pure scientific mind." Why is comedy so difficult to analyze?**

I think because it's like vapor. And the heart of
comedy is how that vapor is suddenly coalesced,
made real all of a sudden by the end stroke. It's
difficult even to describe it. I can't get words around
the feeling. There are so many different kinds of
comedy. There's mild comedy, lovely comedy, like
Booth Tarkington's. Sweet, majestic comedy, like
Sean O'Casey's. Bitter, black comedy like Brendan
Behan's. And there's stand-up wit like Mort Sahl's.

**Max Eastman in his book *The Sense of Humor*
analyzes humor as being derived from pain. He
writes that man is masochistic and enjoys pain in
many forms and that the audience likes to suffer
vicariously. Is that your view?**

No. It is not in our domain, and it's not in the
domain of us geniuses to come up with nomencla-

ture, with handles, or pronunciamentos on comedy. That is for the buff, for the guy who gets very close to it and can't ring the bell. He gets close enough to it at least to surround it with a lot of words. But the magic, the mystery of putting two things together that shouldn't go together and get this special spark called comedy—that we just *do*. And I'm as much in the dark as any bullshit artist about what are the ingredients that make comedy.

Now present me with a comedy sketch, and I'll tell you why it didn't work. But how that sketch came into being is just a bit of a miracle. I could not climb into the glycoproteins that were feeding that part of the brain at that point in the earth's journey around the sun and tell you what happened and how it happened. Some things are buried deep in your unconscious, and suddenly for no good reason you let them fly out at a given time . . . and bang! Something is funny. Who knows why, when, how. Thank God a few people can do it. I could use a few laughs myself.

Some psychologists claim that ideas that come to us intuitively are not "out of the blue" but come as a result of our accumulated knowledge or because of something we may have seen or heard in earlier times.

I agree. I can only agree clinically there are a lot of mechanisms that are operating and that a combination of those forces produces comedy. But I couldn't tell you what the mechanisms are. I agree that there's probably a storehouse of unconscious material. But why we draw on what part of that storehouse is what's miraculous.

And unpinpointable.

A good word. Wonderful. Right.

In *The Funny Men* **Steve Allen wrote: "Some of the funniest jokes are those in which we expect to hear one thing but we hear another." Is this element of surprise the basis for all good comedy construction?**
Not at all. Sometimes comedy is exactly the opposite. Sometimes comedy is wanting to hear something, being tortured into nearly not hearing it and then hearing it. Sometimes good comedy is expecting something to be delivered, having it take a tortuous route and then having it delivered. So there are many ways. Surprise is basic, but it's not all comedy.
There are other techniques?
Yeah. The technique I enjoy is expanding the truth. Truthful situations. Taking real characters and expanding them into fantastic shapes. But in order to do that there has to be a good morsel of truth to begin with.
In *The Great Comedians** **Johnny Carson said, "You can teach formulas for writing but I don't think you can teach somebody to be a Jack Douglas or a Woody Allen. Their minds work in different areas than the normal mind. You don't manufacture a Mel Brooks, It's there. The off-beat mind." Was there anything special in your background that contributed to your being funny?**
Yeah. There may be some simplistic answers that don't really apply. But I'll give you some I think may help. One, I was short, and when I was in public school, pre-teens, I couldn't hang around with the big shots. I couldn't dance, and I couldn't play basketball because I wasn't tall enough. So I needed a

---

*Citadel Press, 1973.

route into the inner circle, into the club, to get my jacket and "Mel" under the pocket and "Royales" or "Diablos" or something on the back of the jacket. I had to get that precious thing. My edge was in amusing them; in making myself invaluable as the block *amusant*, I'd be the source of some kind of comic ice cream for them, a little bit of Jewish dessert. I could buy my way into the inner circle.

The need to be accepted?

Yes. And I think what happens with a lot of comics is they have to be accepted and they overcompensate by becoming massive figures.

You said there were several answers.

Another one could have been pure hate—for the whole world. For being short. For not being born Franklin Roosevelt or Johnny Weismuller—just a lot of hatred. Getting even in an oblique way through comedy instead of just yelling insults and taunts and getting my head smashed in.

The other thing just might be an accident of genes. Maybe it's somebody in my family. My grandmother was very funny, and my mother was very witty. It might just be an accident of chromosomes and genes that gave me a special vocal rhythm or wit. There are many reasons. I said they were simplistic. I really don't know what makes somebody funny.

In a *New York Times* interview with Joanne Stang you said, "My mother had this exuberant joy of living and she infected me with that. She really was responsible for the growth of my imagination." Can you give any specific examples of that statement?

I can't. But she told us stories, and when we were unhappy—crying and bitter—she always managed to somehow jolly us out of it. And I don't know how she did it. And nobody's better than a good comic at doing that.

Then you absorbed that from her?

Yeah. A lot of *The 2000-Year-Old Man* has my mother's vocal rhythms, her rhythms of speech, the words she stressed. My mother had a way of bombastically attacking when she was happy. She'd say, "What're you talkin'?" It's very difficult to explain. I remember she told me that when I was a baby somebody would say to her, "Oh, what a beautiful baby you have!"

And she'd say, "What're you talkin'? *Beautiful!* He's gorgeous!" Almost with anger. I have a lot of that in *The 2000-Year-Old Man.*

That phrasing, that rhythm—isn't that also part of the comedic technique?

Yeah. Phrasing is very important. The hardest thing in writing is to remember how people phrase things—to get down the rhythm of human speech—because when you're writing you tend to write balanced sentences, and people do not speak in balanced sentences. They sometimes skip words, and they make jumps in their head.

They don't always use a verb.

Right. And that doesn't look very good on paper, but it sounds absolutely right. So you've got to change it once again when the actor reads because there's something wrong. So things that look good on paper don't often *sound* good. A writer who has a gift for speech will usually *sound* out a script before it's finished.

In a *Time* magazine story about John Updike, his wife is quoted as saying that early in Updike's career as a staff writer for the *New Yorker* "he thought he'd only be a humorist. He didn't think of

himself as a serious writer." What's the reason for the belief that a humorous writer has less stature than a so-called serious writer?

Because tears have more gravity than laughter. Tears are connected with death and with all the essential tragedy of having been born only to die. So therefore drama, or tragedy, has more weight. Many people don't agree that that's necessarily true, because a fine comedy writer can be a majestic philosopher—Nicolai Gogol, Jonathan Swift. I'm talking about the real comedy writers. Henry Fielding's another.

James Thurber.

In more modern days, Thurber. But I'm talking about the classic writers.

Who wrote humorously?

Yes. Yes.

They made their point just as strongly as Tolstoy or Dostoevski.

Yeah. Sometimes you can make a much stronger point without being lachrymose about it, by doing it obliquely through comedy. You can often discuss tragedy easier and better and get laughs on the way to it.

If a comedian has personal problems and he must go out and perform, at least he's got his act or material to hide behind. The comedy writer must create. Can he still write funny if he's burdened with emotional or psychological disturbances?

Yes and no. Some are lucky enough to use that pressure as a launching pad or to vent a lot of emotion through comedy, and some can't. Some get blocked up and just can't. They have to be happy to write comedy.

Writers have different working habits. Thomas Mann averaged four hundred words a day. Somerset

Maugham, H. G. Wells wrote a thousand. Do you
have a discipline you impose on yourself?
    No. I wish I could. I wish I did. But I don't.
Is it just when you feel like working?
    No. What I do is trap myself. I have gimmicks.
I'll get an idea. I'll write three pages and I'll give it to
somebody, like Warner Brothers, and they'll say,
"We love it," and they'll make a step deal with me.
Once they've given me money, I have to finish it.
What is a step deal?
    That we'll give you so much for a rough draft
and a rough treatment of it and then we'll give you so
much for a finished screenplay, and if we like that,
we'll go on to the movie. So a good method for
comedy writers who are lazy like myself is to trap
themselves with three pages. Now you don't write
the three pages unless you get a terrific idea that
you love. You take those three pages, and if you can't
write further than the three pages—if you say, "OK,
this is good; I've got the whole idea for the screenplay or the play or for the sketch, in three pages"—if
I can't go further, the best thing for me to do now is to
get somebody excited about it. And then that in turn
excites me.
Let's say, for practical purposes, that you turn the
three pages over to your agent or you know somebody. And you send it off. It's in the mail—
    Right. You got it. You make a deal. You're in
trouble. You got to finish it.
But what have you done in the meantime?
    Nothing.
You don't want to do anything?
    I don't want to do a thing. There are exceptions
to that. *The Producers* was a big exception. *The
Producers* I could not stop writing. I did my three
pages and then did another ten-page expansion on

that and then I did a 150-page outline. Then I did 400 pages on that, and I reduced that to 200 pages, and then again I brought it down to a shooting script of 122 pages. I could not stop!

Why?

Those characters just kept writing themselves. Every once in a while there's something you just have to write. It's such fun writing.

Paddy Chayefsky once told me that while he was working, if he got stuck or was having a problem, he read poetry. He said that for him poetry was the best literary form from which to learn clarity as well as brevity. What do you do if you get stuck?

I go into the bathroom and I bang my head against the tiles, and I give myself such a shot—I'm so filled with pain that I decide it's better to sit at a typewriter—I don't sit at a typewriter, by the way— it's better to sit with a pencil and write and more fun than to smash my head against the bathroom tiles and worry and wonder.

Then if you have a block you don't need any outside stimulus?

No. I usually fall down and I'm unconscious for three and a half hours, so what difference does it make? I don't need a thing. All I need is for God to revive me and then I don't do it any more.

Incidentally, I don't use a typewriter. A pencil— it's not gospel when you write it down. You see how scrawly and how stupid-looking it is, and you can always erase it. Somehow when you use a typewriter you fall in love with everything you write. It just looks so good you don't want to tear it up. The typewriter is a big danger, I think, to a writer. I think he should write with a pencil, and then when he's really tired and he can't write anymore, it's a nice device to have your mind still filled. And when your mind gets filled again, it forces you to write even though your hand is cramped—writer's fatigue.

Do you find the quality of the material any different when you're being pressed to meet a deadline compared to what you produce when you're working at a leisurely pace?

Can't give you a good answer. Cannot. Sometimes leisurely I've come up with some sensational things. And sometimes being under the gun has forced me into writing some terrific things, also. Dickens wrote A *Christmas Carol* for money. And only for money. He wasn't even moved by the idea, and he was so intimidated by that he felt guilty about it—he gave it everything he had, and it's one of his best works.

Is it still possible to create funny material even when the creative juices aren't flowing, just through sheer technique?

When you say "creative juices". . . when you're not inspired? When you're not filled? No, I don't think it is. I think you can only write mediocre stuff. I think you have to be filled yourself. And feel it.

What do you do to start those juices going?

I don't know. The idea in your mind. . . the ideas should be the catalytic agents for starting the juices going. I don't think you can start the juices going by running up and down or drinking orange juice.

Or reading poetry?

No. That might be a nice break to clear your head, but it won't inspire you. If I want to take a rest and recharge my batteries, I'll go see a picture like *Kind Hearts and Coronets*, if I can find it. A light, lovely little comedy that I don't think interferes with my kind of comedy and yet tickles and delights me so much I'm ready to go back to work.

The average professional man—a doctor, lawyer, or

engineer—is equipped to practice his skills primarily as a result of training and formal education. Is the craft of comedy writing a technique any intelligent person can learn?

Yes. Any intelligent person can learn it. I think so. Whether he's good at it or not is another question. He can learn it. He can learn some basic rudiments. And the way to learn it is by doing it, and the way to learn best is by doing it professionally, in a room with other writers for a specific show. And for specific talents. Because writing for Alan King is different than writing for Don Rickles or Sid Caesar or Harry Ritz. Harry Ritz is one of my favorite comic personalities.*

Is he one of the comedians you looked up to as a boy?

Yes. Well, I looked up to him because I was always down on the floor laughing. The Three Stooges, Laurel and Hardy, the Ritz Brothers and W. C. Fields were my comic gods. Chaplin didn't thrill me that much. He may have been too artistic for my primitive background.

In the *Times* article with Joanne Stang you said, "The best way to stay alive as a good writer is to run a bulldozer through your conditioned values, learn to live frugally and take all the time you need to develop your ideas. You can't do that if economics are smashing you to the wall." Did you mean that a writer can't do his best work when he's financially strapped?

I think so. I think that if he has to worry about coming up with the rent and with feeding kids, that that is too oppressive to release the muse comfort-

---

*Harry Ritz is one of the Ritz Brothers comedy team, well-known in the thirties and forties on stage and screen.

ably. It would certainly stifle a lot of happy little accidents and insanities that might bloom and flourish

Yet you just pointed out that Dickens was forced to do it.

Yes. But *Christmas Carol* was not a comedy. It was a very serious work, and it had to do with changing moral values, or else he would never make that transition from a poor death into a happy life. For comedy, I think basically you have to feel a little more fired up. More excited and happy. It helps.

Do you have any suggestions or advice to someone interested in becoming a comedy writer?

I'd say learn a trade. I really would. It's a very difficult, competitive job, and I'd say don't do it. Don't ever do it. And if you must do it, against all odds, then maybe you're special and maybe you should. But my advice is not to be a comedy writer!

Art
BUCHWALD

A rthur Buchwald was born in Mount Vernon, New York, on October 20, 1925. His father was a curtain manufacturer, and Arthur's early life was spent in and out of foster homes with his three sisters, Alice, Edith, and Doris. In October 1942, at seventeen, he ran away and joined the United States Marines.

In 1945 Sergeant Buchwald was discharged and enrolled at the University of Southern California. Three years later he departed for France and in due time originated a column, "Paris After Dark," for the European edition of the *New York Herald Tribune.*

In 1951 Buchwald began another column, "Mostly About People," featuring interviews with celebrities in Paris. Later, the two columns were fused into one with the title, "Europe's Lighter Side."

On October 12, 1952, he married Ann McGarry, a former fashion coordinator for Neiman-Marcus. They live in northwest Washington, D.C. with their three adopted children, Joel, Conchita Mathilda, and Marie Jennifer.

Buchwald has done a comedy album for Capitol Records entitled *Sex and the College Boy*. A recent book *I Am Not a Crook,* containing over 125 humorous pieces relating to Watergate, is a hysterical satire of the Washington political scandal that rocked the world.

The following is a partial list of Art Buchwald's published works:

I Never Danced at the White House
Getting High in Government Circles
Have I Ever Lied to You?
Son of the Great Society
And Then I Told the President
I Chose Capitol Punishment
Is It Safe to Drink the Water?
How Much Is That in Dollars?
Don't Forget to Write
More Caviar
Brave Coward
Art Buchwald's Paris
A Gift from the Boys (novel)
Paris after Dark (guide)
Art Buchwald's Secret List to Paris (guide)
The Establishment Is Alive and Well in Washington
Counting Sheep

Art Buchwald's office is in downtown Washington. It is simply furnished—a desk, two chairs, and a small couch. One wall contains shelves of books, mostly on humor, travel, and politics.

Above the bookcase is a picture of Drew Pearson framed in cardboard and a photo of Buchwald in an

Easter Bunny costume. Behind his desk stands an authentic wooden cigar store Indian.

The columnist wore khaki pants, a short-sleeved white shirt, and a black tie with a silver stripe through it. The slight graying at the temples is almost hidden by the black horn-rimmed glasses. Throughout our meeting he sat back in his chair, his feet resting on the desk, and chain-smoked Bering cigars.

Considered by some a caustic humorist, Art Buchwald has also been called a "Will Rogers with chutzpah." But he is not a contrary man. He speaks abruptly and in short sentences, punctuating them with a puckish grin.

This was our conversation:

Before we start, there are some biographical gaps I'd like you to fill in. Can we begin after you graduated from USC in 1948?

I didn't *graduate* from USC. I went there for three years on the GI Bill, and then I discovered you could go to Paris on the GI Bill. I had gotten a two hundred and fifty dollar bonus from New York State for being in the war, and I took the check and bought a one-way ticket to Paris.

You didn't feel it was necessary to finish college?

No. As a matter of fact, I was a *special student* at USC to start with. I had never graduated from high school, so they indicated that I could never get a degree anyway. So I just took what I wanted. I had a ball, and they didn't seem too disturbed by it.

I moved in on the Left Bank with a bunch of guys in a place called the Hotel Des Etats Unis—which means United States—in Montparnasse. This was in '48. We were all ex-GIs, and we decided this was the place to be and the time to be there. We stayed up all night and slept all day. There was a very nice lady at the school we were supposed to go to who marked us "present," so we never got to school much.

What kind of school was it?

It was a language school—the Alliance Française. We saw it a few times, but not too much. It was just a great time to be there. Then I got a little bored with that life, and I got a job stringing for *Variety*—writing space rates, messing around in nightclubs, show business in Paris—for a man who was the *Variety* correspondent. I was sort of his leg man. Then I noticed that the Paris *Herald* didn't have a nightclub column, so I went in and asked them if I could write one, and—

In English?

Yeah, the Paris *Herald* is an English paper. So they hired me to write a nightclub column for twenty-five bucks a week and also to review films. Then I just stayed with it. There were some other columns people dropped out of, so I took them over. Then in 1952 it was syndicated in the States. It was sort of a general feature column which developed into anything I wanted to write about. Then I came back here in '62.

What was the dateline of your first column in the format it's in today?

It's hard to say, because it sort of developed. It was a progression. It started off "Night Clubs." Then I started inserting a little humor. I was a little whimsical with my reviews of films. Then I did a column, "Mostly About People," and it got to be a little more whimsical. It had several titles, and finally it was "Europe's Lighter Side." I forget when that would be—my guess is around '51. But it was a constant development, and there was very little political satire. I didn't do any of that until I got back here.

What do you think were the unique qualifications you possessed to prepare you for this assignment?

Unhappy childhood. I think most of the people you talk to in the humor business had a very unhappy childhood. I once asked George Abbot what he thought made for a creative person and he said, "An unhappy childhood." It makes you go into fantasy very early in life.

In my case, I was a foster child. I was raised in lots of foster homes, and at a very early age I just started turning all this unhappiness into defense humor—which was the greatest defense in the world. This is not something you develop overnight. It's the way you see things. In my case, I'd say, "This is ridiculous!" and turn it into a joke—which I discovered was very socially acceptable. I was the class clown, and I was always in trouble for being the class clown. I was a loner. Being a loner helps. You don't want to become one of the mob. I managed to get people to laugh. That was my way of getting acceptance. I learned very young that if you are a clown, people will be nicer to you.

Having spent your childhood in orphanages, do you think this environment contributed to the shaping of your comedic point of view?

Yes, it was the biggest factor. I'd always been in homes. My mother was dead; my father couldn't raise us; I didn't belong to anybody. I discovered at five or six years old that it was me against the world, and, having discovered that, I had to deal with it. I think I was very much shaped by this life. I don't know how much of this is God-given. You could become a gangster just as easily. I guess underneath it all I was an angry man, and humor is hostility. It's a basic factor. My hostility came out as humor, which was the most socially acceptable form of hostility. Fortunately, I was able to put it on paper.

Then you do go along with Freud's theory that comedy comes from hostility?

Yeah. It did in my case. It's the only explanation I have. There are several psychiatrists who specialize in comedy writers. Humor people are tough on analysts. Humorists are pretty adept at being funny to avoid things that matter.

In a *Newsweek* article you were quoted as saying, "My book is *Catcher in the Rye.*" Is there any particular reason why you identify with the Holden Caulfield character?

He was a loner, and he had all these fantasies which I used to have as a kid. Being shot in the stomach was one I remember. I identified with a guy who was a loner. I think most kids, at least of our generation, were Holden Caulfields whether they wanted to be or not. I used to have all sorts of fantasies. I imagined I was with gangsters . . . there were girls seducing me . . . very identifiable.

During your Marine Corps hitch, did you have any inkling that you would one day write a humor column?

No. I never made plans very far ahead, and I think there is where I was probably very fortunate. If I had tried to plan it, it wouldn't have worked out that way. I was one of these guys who took everything as it came. I ran away from the home to join the marines. I was dumb enough not to realize that there was anything wrong with it—it was fine with me. And here again, I was sort of the comedian of the

whole fighter squadron. I wrote the outfit's newspaper, which was filled with humorous stuff, I
thought. I had no great plan like: "I'm going to be a
writer" or "I'm going to be this." It was just that the
marines was that part of my life; USC was that part
of my life; then Europe. I never made any really
serious plans about it.

**Do you think funnier today than you did twenty or
thirty years ago—during this gestation period?**

No, I don't think funnier, but after twenty years
at this you recognize things that lead to humor more
easily.

**Because of the experience, do you think you express
it or write it better?**

I would say so. I hope so. I don't consider I've
ever written the perfect column. I've got a lot of
things to do yet. I want to write a novel. I want to
write a play. I don't even consider that I've started
yet. My dream now is to be Neil Simon. He gets all
those royalties.

**Would you describe the step-by-step process in
putting together one column?**

OK. As you see, on my desk I have clippings
here from different newspapers. Here's one:
"Namath Has Judgment To Make." I don't know
what I'm going to do with Namath yet. I've got
Namath on my mind. Here's one about Saigon where
they are investigating opposition groups, and I cut
one out here about this guy in the Pentagon who got
hell because he told the truth about—

**Then it begins with your clipping out ideas you feel
would made for a good column.**

Right. Something preferably that everybody
knows about so I don't have to devote any of the
column to explaining the situation. I have only
about six hundred words. If I have to take up half the

column with explanation and then comment on it, it takes too long. So I prefer a story that people are aware of that would take up only the first paragraph.

I'll give you an example of one I did. I read in the paper that Mrs. Rose Kennedy had called up Senator [Everett] Dirksen after Dirksen had attacked Teddy Kennedy in the Senate. She wanted to thank him for being so moderate and generous about Teddy. Well, Dirksen was flabbergasted. What can you say when a mother compliments you on attacking her son? I filed this away. I didn't have any use for it at that moment. Then [Strom] Thurmond attacked Teddy Kennedy about five days later in the Senate, and it was a very tough exchange. So I thought to myself, What will happen when Rose Kennedy calls up Thurmond? So I did a kind of fantasy article about a telephone call from Rose Kennedy to Thurmond thanking him for being so kind to Teddy. And at the end of the article, he calls up Dirksen and says, "We've been had!"

Then step one is your clipping.

No; step one is *reading* the newspaper—seeing something there that I file away in my mind. Step two is getting a news peg for the situation, getting a reason for it. Step three is developing it on the typewriter. A lot of times step three turns out much different than I imagined when I started, because I will get an idea and then I'll see it doesn't work, or I'll get one line in the column which will just send me off on another tack which is much better.

Do you often *overwrite* to get the six hundred words?

No; my typewriter practically stops at six hundred words automatically.

Do you have a basic framework that you use?

I like dialogue. I prefer to do it in forms of skits. I like the reader to use his mind—*his* imagination. Like I might say, "I went to the Pentagon's department on keeping costs up . . ." Then it's an interview with that man in that department in the Pentagon. I might describe his office or something. Now the reader is with me. He's at the actual spot where it is taking place, which gives a reality to a fantasy thing. People laugh, and they know it's true, and they know it's not true. Now that kind of formula works best for me. Sometimes I might do straight commentary, which works, but I find that the ones that have a skit work best for me.

Is this format something you started with right from the beginning?

No; I think it probably evolved. First, in writing humor for newspapers you have to get the confidence of the reader. If he doesn't know who you are he gets very suspicious, and he gets very resentful of you if you are going to be funny. So it takes time to build up your audience. Once the audience is on your side and they accept you, they'll take anything from you. This is the reason there are very few people writing humor in the newspapers. First, nobody lets them develop, and an editor doesn't have the patience to let a guy find his own level. Secondly, the reader becomes very resentful of a guy they don't know being funny. It's a very limited business. There are only about three or four of us in it.

Aside from your putting away ideas in your mind for later, how long does it take to write the actual column?

About one hour.

From the moment you sit down?

Yeah. If I get lucky—faster.

How many columns a year?

Three a week—fifty-two weeks a year.

When you finish a column, to what degree can you predict whether or not that piece is uncommonly funny?

It's almost impossible. On the ones I think are brilliant I get no reaction at all. The ones I'm a-shamed of and I'm sorry I handed in I get a tremendous reaction on. It's so unpredictable—which is probably healthy, because if I knew what worked I might stay with it and then it could get tiresome. The thing about any kind of comedy or humor is this: The one thing that can do you in is predictability. If the audience can predict how you're going to treat it and how you're going to handle it, then you're old hat. What you have to be doing constantly—and this is true of all comedians—is to *be* in such a way that they can't predict what you are up to. It's the surprise factor.

What standards or criteria of taste do you set for yourself?

Well, I know I'm writing for a newspaper audience, so I would write differently than I do for *Playboy*—which I write for occasionally. I assume that everyone is going to read it—kids and wives and editors who are very sensitive. I have about 450 papers. A lot of them are in small towns where they are a little more nervous about things. So I try not to be off-color, mainly because when I have something to say—like on the subject of sex education—I want to get it in the paper and I don't want them to be watching for me to slip stuff in.

My style is different from a lot of comedians in

that I don't go for the jugular and, if I do, I try to sugarcoat it. And people will take it from me because they're not afraid of me. There are some comedians that people are actually afraid of. They're scared of them. They'll laugh at them, but they're afraid of them. I'm a little more subversive about it. I try to sneak in. I'm their pal.

You try to do it more subtly.

You do it subtly and you pretend you're on their side. And you do it in such a way that even people you're hitting the hardest can't point their finger and say, "What did you do to me?" You say, "What do you mean, what did I do to you?" There's a sort of innocence about it.

I also find some subjects harder to deal with than others. Obviously the race question is the toughest. It's in an area I will comment on, but I find it's very hard to do because I myself am not sure of the whole thing. When we were all for integration it was great, but now since the black militants are for black and we're for white—and I'm against that kind of separation—I find myself in a spot. I find that's one of the few areas that's hard to touch. Most of the rest of the stuff, even religion, is not that difficult anymore.

Is there any special theme or topic that lends itself to being particularly funny subject matter?

Well, big government obviously does. The executive branch of government did—more under Johnson than under Nixon. People were afraid of Johnson. Therefore Johnson was a perfect foil, just like De Gaulle. They were both beautiful people for a humorist. The Pentagon obviously is good. The CIA. The things that people are afraid of are the best things to sock it to. Now the areas where I don't feel you're being very brave are attacking the Pentagon or attacking the CIA or even the administration. But the areas where you are really in trouble is making fun of the left—which you have to do, because the extreme left is very ridiculous now, just as the extreme right is. But when you make fun of the left you find all the people who believed in you suddenly turn against you and say you sold out and everything. That's where it takes a little more guts.

Do you write to please yourself or the reader?

Myself. I really do. I don't try and think in terms of what the reader reaction is going to be. I really write for myself. I even laugh at my own stuff.

Is politics the subject you've written most about?

No; the subjects I've written most about are mores, social comment—on everything. Politics is a good springbroad for many pieces, but it doesn't. . . I don't stay with it. People are far more interested in things that have nothing to do with politics. I'll get more mail if I write about the Vatican kicking St. Christopher off the calendar than I will about any political story. I'll get more mail on a thing I did on American Express and computers than I will the IBM. So if you write about things that people feel about and know about and have something to do with, you get more mail and more reaction.

Whenever you've written about a narrow moral concept or social injustice, has that column helped change or alter opinion?

I don't think so. Somebody did a study on it. A professor asked me if he could take some columns and see if people's minds could be changed before and after they read them. It was at Southern Illinois, I think. He sent me the results, and I don't think there was that much change. It had to do with the recognition of Red China.

My function, if I have one, is making a living and enjoying my work—is sort of taking some of the steam out of everything. This is a very uptight country now, and everybody is kind of uptight. So if you can take some of the pressure off, maybe you are doing a bigger service than changing things.
You said "making a living." Is that your primary concern?

It's not my *primary* concern. I just wanted to point out that I have to make a living whether it's doing this or something else. I like what I'm doing, so it works well together.
What about the pressure of coming up with a column three times a week? How does it affect your personal life?

I don't find it much of a pressure. My pressures come from other things. They come from family— things I have to deal with which I don't understand. They come from a tremendous amount of mail— requests to make appearances . . . for charities . . . all the stuff that goes with the column. That's where the pressure is. The column's a snap. I love it.
Were there any courses you took at college that you feel helped prepare you to write funny?

No; it's a course in life. To be funny is something that doesn't come out of school at all. School might help you polish your English or something so you can put it down in words, but I had much better experience. I was managing editor of a humor magazine at USC. I was a columnist at USC. I wrote a variety show, and I found that was far more useful to me than courses I took. I took them, but I don't know if they helped me or not.
At the beginning did you study Thurber or Benchley or Perelman or any of the other humorists?

I didn't study them; I *read* them—Ring Lardner

particularly. But then I discovered—I guess it was when I started writing on the *Herald Tribune*—that there wasn't a new idea under the sun, that everyone had thought of it before I did. So I stopped reading these guys so I wouldn't be inhibited by anything *they* wrote.

Bill Boggs, the editor of the Miami *News*, said that your humor "puts things in perspective." Is it possible to make light of a serious subject and expect people to see it more clearly?

I think what you get when you write something that people laugh at is the recognition that they think the same way only they haven't been able to say it. I have people say to me constantly, "Why didn't I think of that?" I don't know where it comes from, the ability to do that. I did one that hit home to a lot of people. That was when Johnson was doing a lot of things in Viet Nam. I wrote a piece about having a nightmare in which Barry Goldwater had been elected president of the United States—he was bombing Viet Nam, and he was defoliating. And when I said I had this nightmare, I was saying all the things that *Johnson* was really doing at the time. And I said, "I woke up and, thank God, Johnson was President of the U.S."

A lot of people had forgotten it, but Johnson was more or less following all the things that Goldwater had advocated. This got them very mad at the White House. Johnson denied it.

These things just occur to me as sort of an automatic reflex. I read here [*pointing to clipping*] that "Four of Opposition Group in Saigon Are Summoned to the Police Inquiry." This is an opposition government in Saigon who think they should have government reconciliations. So it looks like they are going to be arrested. When I read this, I said, "Whoop! Here we are fighting for this great country called South Viet Nam, and they are arresting everybody and closing newspapers." I've written that column before, unfortunately, but maybe I can find another way of saying it.

There's the sense of the ridiculous about this [*pointing to another clipping*]: This guy in the Pentagon—he found out they were charging too much for stuff. Instead of getting a promotion they kicked him out. This is the kind of stuff that is going on every day. Your front page is where the humor is being written—not the columns.

In the Newsweek **story I mentioned earlier you were characterized as a man who "harpooned the heart of the U.S. policy," a "court jester in residence," and "one of the best satirists of our time." Do these critical comments agree with your own view of your work?**

I like them. I like when poeple say those things. I'll be very honest to say this: I don't really think of myself as a satirist. People say, "What do you want to be described as?" when they're going to introduce me. I say, "A columnist." I don't want a heavy label on me which I'll be stuck with or have to hang on to. At the same time, you find that as the quality of your stuff—if it gets better—you're making it harder for yourself because you have to keep it going.

Keep topping it.

Yeah. At least not fall below. So you're your own worst enemy in a sense, because the better you get the tougher it gets. So you can't relax. So I accept compliments. I had to go through two and one-half years of analysts before I could accept compliments. I imagine most of the people you talk to have been in analysis.

Many comedians also.

Because we're not set up to accept success. One of the toughest things to handle in life for somebody who has had a rough life is success. You've been kicked around when you were a kid so you get used to that and you know you *should* be kicked around. To be on top is a very difficult thing—not to let it scare you, because it scares the hell out of you. You know you don't want to be there, and your whole life has been a series of preparations for the worst.

Newsweek also described you as being an "elaborately naive analyst who takes complex woes of the world and reduces them to their logical absurdities." Is that also a correct analysis of your approach to laughter?

Yes, that's what I try to do and in as simple terms as possible. That's the whole gist of it. If you were to ask me to describe the column I would say, "It's a political cartoon in words." I consider myself a political cartoonist who can't draw.

Even though politics is not the subject you write most about?

Yeah, but most of your poltical cartoonists don't stick to politics. They're dealing with Americana too. I don't know where politics starts and stops. Is Ralph Nader politics; Is "auto safety" politics?

You wouldn't call your comedy *satire* then?

No, I wouldn't label it. People label it what they want. Everybody has to put a label on everything. If that's what they want to call it, fine.

How about "truth stretched for comedic purposes"?

I think the *Newsweek* description is better. To take a complex thing and simplify it and carry it to

its extreme—maybe that's satire. I don't know. I'm
not well versed in what all the terms are. I really
don't know too much about humor except that it's a
mystery and it's like sex—you don't want to know
too much about it. I never read any books on sex,
either.

**Newsweek also called you the "funniest newspaper
columnist and one of the nation's sharpest political
satirists." Is the definition of a political satirist
simply one who pokes fun at politics?**

I don't know. We're back to definitions, and I'm
not good at them. A humorist may poke fun, or he
may make a point. It's saying something that's been
said before but saying it differently.

And *funny.*

Funny to the audience. That's why you cannot
say—if you write something and people don't think
it's funny—that it's "funny." There's nobody to
judge that except the reader. And you can't shove
things down their throats. This is true of comedians.
You can't get up there and try a joke and if it doesn't
work say, "You don't know anything!" I don't know
what my audience considers funny, but as long as
you're on the same wavelengths, you're in business.
Mort Sahl got off the wavelength for a while there.

**Mort Sahl is considered a political satirist, and
naturally he** *verbalizes* **his satire. What's the difference in the approach to making people laugh
through written humor as compared to the spoken
joke?**

Mort Sahl has sort of a machine-gun delivery—
you gotta be really on your toes to get it. You have to
be listening real hard. Now a column people can
read slow or fast. If they didn't get it, they can even
go back to it.

I do a lot of lectures, and my delivery can have a

big effect on the laugh. I can say something in a very funny way, and it could help the laugh by maybe fifty percent. When it's in cold print, the humor depends on the content. There's no delivery to help you. So I would say the big difference between a comedian and somebody who writes humor is that when you write it you don't have the delivery going for you, and you don't have your personality going for you.

And the personal contact.

Right. If there are four really good laughers in an audience, then everybody else comes in. If the room is wide, you get less laughter because people feel nervous. But if they're all close together in a theater, they feel safe. But I have people tell me they are sitting on a train reading my column and they laugh out loud and the other people think they are nuts. It's really harder to make people laugh with the written word than the spoken word, because delivery plays a great part in jokes.

How about on your lecture dates? Do you use the material from your columns?

Yes.

Does it evoke big laughter?

Yes. People recognize it, and it doesn't seem to bother them. I do one, for example, where I say, "I read an article where there would soon be a pill for women who are over sixty to have children. So I went to see my Aunt Molly and said, 'Aunt Molly, they've just invented a pill which makes it possible for a woman over sixty to have a baby.'

"And she said, 'Wash your mouth out with soap and water.'

"I said, 'Just think: A woman of sixty can soon have a child!'

"She said, 'If your Uncle Leo so much as lays a finger on me, I'll hit him with a chair.'"

"I said, 'But you can help us in the cold war against China.'

"She said, 'I'm not interested in having kids at my age even if they give it to us free under Medicare.'" This one is really hysterical and people laugh.

Is there one particular column that is a personal favorite?

Well, there a few I kind of enjoyed. One is: I wrote that there was no J. Edgar Hoover—that he had been invented by the *Reader's Digest*. The whole column had to do with the idea that there had been twenty-six J. Edgar Hoovers and the picture you saw of him was a composite of all the FBI agents. I got more reaction from people who believed it. It was really funny, because people wrote to the *Reader's Digest*, and they wrote to the FBI. It was the funniest thing— the reaction on it. I did it deadpan, and it worked like a dream. I got a charge out of that one.

Many newspapermen, novelists, and playwrights feel that as the world becomes grimmer it is increasingly more difficult to appeal to the public's sense of humor. Has this been your experience?

No; that's a cop-out. The challenge of a person who is doing this work is to make people laugh. I don't think the ones who are doing it feel this way. The people who feel this way are the people who are not succeeding at it. If you're succeeding, you don't blame the public. If my column doesn't work, it's not because of them. My articles appear in about a hundred different papers throughout the world besides about three hundred and fifty in the states, in every language—Japanese, Russian, Chinese,

Spanish. They're appealing to people who have entirely different setups than we do. I get mail from them.

It's a beautiful business, because you can make people happy. And there are very few people in this world that have a chance to make other people happy. If you can make people laugh, they like you; you're everybody's friend. It's a nice feeling to know you can make people laugh, and it also has a certain amount of power to it. I go through life; I meet people. Everywhere I go, I'm well received. It's probably subconsciously what I was going for all my life. Now that I'm achieving it, I'm enjoying it.

Abe
BURROWS

A braham S. Burrows was born in New York City on December 18, 1910. His father was a retailer of wallpaper and paints. Abe graduated from Brooklyn's Utrecht High School (1928), then attended the College of the City of New York (1928-29) and New York University (1929-32).

The "Sage of Shubert Alley" began his professional career as a radio writer for the program "This Is New York" (1938). Then he wrote for the Texaco Star Theatre (1939), "The Rudy Vallee Show" (1940), "Duffy's Tavern" (1940-1945), "The Dinah Shore Show" (1945), "The Joan Davis Show" (1945), and "The Abe Burrows Show" (1946-1947), in which he starred.

Abe Burrows wrote the screenplay for *The Solid Gold Cadillac* and has innumerable credits as a writer and performer in television. But it is in the Broadway theater that he has received world recognition—as a writer, composer, lyricist, and director. Here is a partial list of the stage shows with which Abe Burrows has been associated:

Forty Carats (director)
Cactus Flower (author and director)

What Makes Sammy Run (director)
How to Succeed in Business without Really Trying (director and coauthor of book with Jack Weinstock and Willie Gilbert; received New York Drama Critics and Antoinette Perry Awards and the Pulitzer Prize in Drama)
Say Darling (director and coauthor of book with Richard and Marion Bissell)
Happy Hunting (director)
Silk Stockings (coauthor of book with George S. Kaufman and Leueen MacGrath)
Can Can (writer and director)
Two on the Aisle (director)
Guys and Dolls (coauthor of book with Joe Swerling; received New York Drama Critics and Antoinette Perry Awards)

In 1959 Abe Burrows married Carie Eloise Smith. They have two children, James Edward and Laurie Ellen.

This talk was recorded at Abe Burrows's New York apartment. He greeted me warmly at the door and led the way through a cavernous foyer lined with books and paintings to a small sitting-room/office. On the walls were photographs of some of the most important theatrical figures of our time—all close associates of the man I came to interview.

Abe Burrows is over six feet tall and solidly built. He is balding and wears heavy, flesh-colored glasses. He had on a green-checked sport shirt, a tan corduroy jacket, and brown slacks. He chain-smoked throughout my stay.

An incredible metamorphosis seems to take

place in Abe Burrows after one meets him. At first
impression his harsh voice makes him appear gruff
and intimidating. But within minutes it becomes
obvious how wrong instant judgments can be. Burrows exudes genuine kindness and gentility. Anxious to share his knowledge, desirous of passing on
what he has learned, his attitude is almost
rabbinical.

After college your first job was on Wall Street.

Yes; I worked for a brokerage firm. I was a
runner, a board boy, and a wire clerk—and a custom-
er's man. While I was doing that I was studying
accounting at night, and then I was an accountant in
'33 or '34.

Did you have any desire to write comedy then?

No. I'm not one of the guys who always dreamt
of being a writer. I was a funny guy. I played piano
and entertained at parties, but I never had any ideas
of writing comedy then, I'm one of the few people
who'll admit I went into comedy writing for money. I
was broke. It was 1937 when I started. I was married
and having money troubles. There were no jobs, and
I found out you could get paid for selling jokes. I
joined up with Frank Gallin—he since passed
away—and we were partners for about two years.
We sold jokes to Henny Youngman, Eddie Garr.
Eddie was the first man to do our stuff on the air.
He's dead, too. He was one of the great mimics. When
he did Durante he *looked* like him.

How did you learn the technique of writing jokes?

I never learned the technique. It's like hitting in
baseball; you either can or you can't. You can teach a
lot of things. You can teach taste, editorial sense, but
the ability to say something funny is something I've
never been able to teach anyone. I had a class out in

California for a while. I've *lectured* at UCLA in comedy writing, but I never *taught* it. You can teach a person how to edit a joke or how to pass up a bum joke, but you can't make him think funny.

You say you can teach someone to "pass up a bum joke." Doesn't that come from experience?

Yeah. College kids send me stuff that almost always has what I call "baby" jokes. I used to tell young students and writers, "If it's the kind of a joke your kid brother could have thought up, don't do it." After a while, a joke or a pun occurs to you and you realize that probably everybody else thought of it, too.

You say you never learned the technique. There must be some jokes that you know work for you, that have a certain formula.

After a while, when you've written a long time and you've been around jokes, you can say, "Here's the kind of joke that might fit here!" Then you might switch it.

What do you mean by "switch it"?

Oh, change it from a streetcar to a motorcycle.

While you were at college did you take any writing courses?

Nope, I took a lot of English literature. I was always an avid reader. I was always hungry for books. I hated to have them used up.

Did you concentrate on humor books?

No; I read everything. I was a compulsive reader. If I was out of something to read, I would read the directions on the back of a soap powder box. To this day, if I get on a plane, I take enough stuff to last me around the world. I'm always afraid of running out of stuff to read. I was always *word*-oriented.

Robert Benchley was very word-oriented. His son, Nathaniel, wrote his biography and said that while his father was at Harvard, he learned ten new words a day. He forced himself to go to the dictionary.

Actually, he didn't force himself; he loved it. I read the dictionary steadily. I used to be a scholar. My ambition was not writing. I wanted to teach Latin. I studied Latin for about seven years—four in high school and three years in college. As a matter of fact, years ago I did a program on television and radio called "We Take Your Word" with Lyman Bryson. We worked on definitions and derivations of words. A lot of it was based on my Latin training. I still consider myself sort of a Latinist.

Isn't the affection for words, the keen interest in them, part of a comedy writer's tools?

Today it's a must. You can't turn out good dialogue without it. Too many of the writers today don't have the words, especially for the large amount of stuff they need for television. I hear constant errors in grammar, wrong uses of words, lack of words. The kids don't have enough words because they don't read enough.

At the beginning, were there any men other than Frank Gallin who influenced or helped you develop your talent?

The biggest influence at that time was Ed Gardner. I was the head writer of "Duffy's Tavern." This was around 1940.

Then you became fairly successful rather quickly.

Immediately.

In a field you had not intended to go into and had not studied for.

I use that as a lesson for young guys, frequently. I was twenty-seven when I became a writer professionally, and I was ready. I was a very well-read, educated fellow with a good sense of taste, and I did well instantly. What Ed Gardner did for me was this: He was not really a writer himself. He was a good director, a great editor, and he had a tremendous sense of taste. The Talmud says, "A man should do two things for himself: Pick out a good friend and pick out a teacher." I was very lucky. I had two great teachers. My first one, in radio, was Ed Gardner. The second I met when I went into the theater. My first show was *Guys and Dolls*, and my first director was George Kaufman. They were the two most important guys in my professional life.

In what way did Gardner coach you?

He'd rap me across the knuckles. I'd write a line; it seemed to be all right—"Here he comes now . . ."

He'd say, "Come on, Abe; you can't say that!"

I'd say, "Why not?"

"It's just wrong." After a while his taste began to be ingrained. I'd recognize the *corny* line, the *obvious* line, the *dull* line, the *vulgar* line.

How about George S. Kaufman?

He did the same thing for me in a different way. After years of writing for television and radio I found I was taking the easy path; that is, when you've got to do a show a week, you can't take the time to polish, comb for the good things, You put down the first thing that occurs to you. It's four o'clock in the morning; you need the script that morning at ten o'clock; you do it. With Kaufman, he would look at a couple of pages of mine and he'd point out a joke and say, "Abe, that's too easy!" It was a dreadful thing for me to hear, because he was right. I put down the first thing that occurred to me— some topical line.

To this day, when they make jokes about the Los

Angeles Freeway—that's too easy. Everybody does it. "We need a laugh here; let's do a joke about the freeway." In my day, it was the La Brea Tar Pits; it was Eddie Cantor's children. And about things like that Kaufman would say, "Too easy!" for a moment I balked, and I then understood. I remember I had a joke in *Guys and Dolls* that I repeated twice. He said to me, "Abe, you did that joke earlier."

I said, "We have that in radio, George. That's what we call a running gag."

He said, "Those people are paying $6.50. Give 'em a new joke."

Is it possible to put your finger on the psychological factors that motivated you to want to write comedy?

Oh, there are a lot of them. Humor is a way to keep from killing yourself. When you look at things, dreadful things with a funny slant, it removes your anxiety. It really keeps you from killing yourself, in the broad sense of the word.

Are you saying, then, that when you got out of school things were so bad you were thinking of killing yourself?

Things are always difficult for every kid. It's how you *look* at it. How do you *cope* with life? Other kids used to throw rocks; I made jokes. Even private little jokes to myself. If I was mad at my father or my mother I made jokes about them in my mind. When I was running around trying to get a job, struggling, I saw little quirks, and the guys who would ordinarily terrify me looked silly. When I did *How to Succeed in Business*—those were all the silly guys I had trouble getting work from.

Is there anything in your background or your environment that you feel made you decide to write comedy?

I didn't *decide* to write comedy; I *began* to write

comedy. Big difference. I found that I could. It's very hard to decide to write comedy. It's pathetic to see people who really can't cope with it *trying* to write comedy. There's a writer still around who, when he thinks of a joke, writes it in a book and saves it for his second act curtain. Real writers don't do it that way. It comes when you need it. We know it and we trust it as a way of life. It's like throwing a forward pass. You don't *decide* to learn how to throw a forward pass. You find you can throw a pass and you learn how to do it well, and then instinctively do it when you have to. I am still able to come up with a punch line when I need it.

You see, when you are talking about comedy now, you are only talking about jokes, which, of course, are the essence, whether you are Molière or Shakespeare or "Doc" Simon. But the whole thing can be a joke. The whole play has a funny aura which they call situation comedy. Of course, every time you pull the trigger and you make the audience laugh, you've made a joke.

In a panel discussion, "What Can We Expect from Broadway," with you, Harold Prince, Jerome Weidman, and Walter Kerr, Kerr said, "A good writer of comedy is himself as serious as anyone else." What characteristics then differentiate the comedy writer from anyone else?

It's his way of looking at things—his way of coping. Let's get back to my earlier statement: "Some kids threw rocks; I made jokes!" A guy faces the world today; he looks at it. James Reston sits down and writes a profound, serious analysis. Art Buchwald looks at exactly the same thing, thinks the same way about it as Reston does, has the same opinions; yet Buchwald cloaks his in comedy. That's

his way of coping. It's his *language*—you might put it
that way. Some people accuse comedy writers of
copping out. Maybe it's true. They're afraid to state it
seriously. They state it with a laugh so no one will be
offended. It probably isn't in the big sense a cop-out,
but then breathing is a cop-out too.

**Why isn't the comedy writer's product accepted on
the same high plane as the serious writer's?**

Because humor is considered levity, and we're a
puritanical nation. If you're not serious, if you're
laughing, it's considered levity, and levity is infe-
rior. They say, "That's silly." The word *silly, capri-
cious, levity* is the great insult. They say you can't
be any good if you laugh. In church, you're not
supposed to make jokes. During a deadly serious
church service nobody would dare make a joke. A
joke would kill the magic, would upset God. In
Fiddler on the Roof, Sholem Aleichem did that, and
religious people were shocked. He had Tevye, the
hero of *Fiddler,* talking to God, and that was considered very bad form.

But excellent stage form.

Yeah, after a while people began to accept it. A
lot of people are still offended by it, think it's not
nice. I wrote a guest piece once for Walter Kerr in
which I told why I was so pleased that *How to
Succeed in Business without Really Trying* got the
Pulitzer Prize. Walt suggested the title "Why I Did
Not Turn Down the Pulitzer Prize." I said, "It was a
tribute to comedy." I know it was a serious play.
People came in hushed and treated it with huge
respect. If it's a comedy they come in chattering and
they say, "Abe, very funny, very funny," and they
dismiss it.

I claim with comedy we make much more

serious points than we do with anything that's supposed to be serious. See, a laugh is one of the most profound things that can happen to a human being. When you make a man laugh, you have evidently hit him right where he lives—deep. You've done something universal. You've moved him in an area that he probably didn't dare even think about, and he laughs explosively.

Now laughter is a dangerous thing. You are helpless when you laugh. Lean back and you're exposing yourself to people around you. You're making a loud, rude noise—which is what a laugh is. You can be assassinated when you're laughing; you're that helpless. Now to evoke a reaction like that you must have said something very deep.

Particularly if you have a thousand people in a group and they are all laughing or the majority are laughing at the same time.

That's right. So you've done *something* universal. As far as a tear, I've seen people cry at Christmas cards or at some fool quoting poetry on television. I've seen people moved by a tiny love song. But a laugh, a real belly—wow! I don't mean a smile, which is based on a clever play on words; I mean a VOOM! You've done something there. Perhaps that very thing is what causes people to say, "Well, it's ridiculous; it doesn't mean anything!" When they see real truth they flee from it.

In that same panel discussion you said, "I write serious plays but they come out funny. They get laughs but the subject matter is always serious." Did you mean that you didn't consciously write to evoke laughter?

Well, the question I'm always asked on lecture tours is, "Haven't you ever wanted to do anything serious?" And I say, "Everything I do is serious, but it comes out funny." That is my approach. I give myself to it. I expect laughter because I'm thinking funny. I'm in trouble when I say, "I haven't gotten a laugh here; I better shove one in." That's when every comedy writer is in trouble. But if the dialogue isn't coming out funny, there's something wrong with the machinery.

Is there anything a writer can do to oil up the machinery when it's not working?

Usually if it's not working he's on a bum subject. It may be a subject about which he cannot be funny. I've said, "I just can't be funny about this war, or the atom bomb. I can't think funny." I couldn't think funny about Hitler. A lot of guys did funny jokes about the Nazis. I couldn't. It just didn't come up. But to me, that is the essence of the good, natural comedy writer. It has to come naturally to him. If he's forcing, he's no good.

In that same panel discussion you also said, "One of my goals as a playwright of comedy is to send the audience out feeling complete—satisfied." Would you explain that?

There are a lot of plays in the theater today—and always have been—that are designed to dig up a tough situation and leave it unresolved. The author wants the audience to be upset by it. I've actually heard guys say, "I want them to go out upset and worried." I don't say that's an unworthy motive. I just don't work that way. I like to send them out feeling better than when they came in. I *like* them to be thinking. I like everything I say on paper to have some *meaning*. I don't like it to be about *nothing*. *How to Succeed in Business without Really Trying* is very serious. It's about ruthless, ambitious guys in a certain form of business. The main character was a killer. At the end I treated it amusingly, and people went out kind of happy with what happened but *thinking*.

You believe in the happy ending.

Not the *happy* ending, the *complete* one. *Hamlet* has a complete ending. Four people are dead on that stage. Hamlet, the queen, the king, and Laertes— Ophelia died earlier. They're all dead, and Horatio leans over Hamlet and says, "Good night, sweet Prince," and you get goose pimples. There's a completion as they pick up Hamlet's body and carry it off to the battlements. I think the word is "satisfying" rather than "happy." I like a *satisfying* ending. I don't like plays where the curtain comes down, the ending is just a punch line, and the audience says, "Is it over?" I've had that experience watching hit plays.

Why is writing to evoke laughter more difficult than creating a so-called serious play?

I don't know if it's *more* difficult. I think the problem is that the guys who try to write comedy and find it *difficult* are not funny. I know serious playwrights who treasure a laugh or two when they get it because they're not guys who think that way. It isn't a matter of *more difficult*. It'd probably be just as difficult for *me* to turn around and say, "I'm going to have a play tomorrow which is going to be a good play and not a laugh in it!" That's tough. As I said before, you can either do it or you can't.

The most pathetic thing—you've seen it at parties—the man who makes jokes all the time. He's not funny, and you know he's not going to get better. He might hire some comedy writers to give him party material, but he just doesn't understand the *whys* of comedy. I've had people say to me, "You don't like anybody else's jokes." I'm a good audience. I hate bum jokes. I hate sweat jokes. I hate to see guys trying who are not funny. Guys are funny or they're not; that's all.

It divides up that way among comedians. There are comedians who have great material, but they're not funny without it. There is the comic fellow who walks out, says, "Hello!" and you fall down. Other guys—if they have a clever joke, it goes; if not, they lay there. A good comedian never lays there.

Charlie Chaplin, in his autobiography, defines humor as "the subtle discrepancy we discuss in what appears to be normal behavior." Can that definition be used as the foundation for creating all funny dialogue?

Well, if you think of that as the foundation, you are not going to think of anything funny. I use a more simple thing to define the construction of humor. I use baseball terms. I call a joke a curve. See, a curve is a ball that starts out to the plate, and then it bends to fool the batter. That's exactly what you do with a comedy line and the audience. You throw what seems to be a perfectly straight line and then curve it. It curves right at the end, usually. The good ones do.

The oldest one of all: "Who was that lady I saw you with last night?" "That was no lady. That was my wife!" Till the guy says, "That was my wife!" his curve doesn't break. I'll say to an actor, "Pull the string on it." That's a way of delivering a line. When you throw your line you delay it; you do it faster. So when Chaplin says "the subtle discrepancy," what it is, is that he's showing you a perfectly straight, seemingly straight thing, and suddenly there's a hole in it. "Curve" is the best way to describe a joke. **I remember a playwriting course I took at college, the professor said to write "what you're familiar with." Has everything you've written been based on that concept?**

I find I'm much better with things I'm at home with; otherwise I'm in strange territory. A fellow with a good sense of humor can be much funnier when he's in familiar surroundings, with people who understand him, people he understands. My French is very poor. When I'm in Paris I can get by, but I can't make jokes. I'm no wit in Paris. When I do get a laugh in French I'm delighted. I go out of my mind with joy. Wit doesn't travel.

The great Hungarian playwrights of the twenties came to Hollywood in the thirties and the wits were in terrible trouble. They couldn't make it. They were funny in Budapest; in Hollywood they weren't funny. [Ferenc] Molnar was really great in this country. He "traveled" because the men who adapted his plays were great playwrights themselves and witty. Robert Sherwood, Daryl Langden Stuart. So if you're out of your element you're not going to be funny.

A couple of times I have gone into costume things and haven't been successful at them. The critics won't accept them from me. One guy who had given me a rave for a show some time ago said, "Now I can forgive Abe for that costume thing he did two years ago." It's best to stay where you know you're at home. It seems almost a truism: What's the sense of writing about something you don't know anything about? Why write it?

How to Succeed **was an enormous theatrical effort to**

produce. What is the step-by-step process in putting together a musical comedy?

I start with the music. I sat with Frank Loesser, for instance, and we figured out where the music was going to go. A lot of people think you go for the book first in a musical. That's silly. You have to find things that the composer can say in music. I'd say to Frank, "What can we do here in an office that's musical; What can we say?" He and I sat together, and we came up with about eight musical numbers before I even started writing the book.

You said to Loesser, "What can we do in an office?" Then you had some idea of where you were going?

Oh, we had a layout, yeah. Not the dialogue. Not the scene breakdown. I find it better to build towards songs than to have the songs just come out. I get books all the time in which the author writes: "Here will be a song that all the gypsies will sing." That's deadly. First of all, the composer is the key man in a musical. There's an anomaly there. The *book* is the most important, and the *songs* are the most important. Now you figure where it goes from there. It's harder to do a song than to write a scene.

Let's take *How to Succeed* from the beginning.

How to Succeed in Business without Really Trying was sort of a satiric guide book [by Shepherd Mead]. Jack Weinstock and Willie Gilbert did an adaptation. They wanted to do it as a straight play. Frank Loesser and I took all this material, and we started from scratch. We began with: Where could you sing in an office; The first idea Frank had for a song was "Coffee Break." We pictured all these people singing about coffee in the office, and that really kicked us off. Then we got an idea for an opening. Then we got about five more song spots. **So each musical number began to take form in terms of music and lyric before you began writing the book?** That's right. Frank and I would work separately, then come together. It sort of grows like a ball of wax. Then as a comedy director I think on my feet a lot. Frequently, before a rehearsal, I will leave a scene very sketchy. Four or five of the biggest scenes in *How to Succeed* were largely developed while I was on my feet working with the actors. I had a general idea where they would go and most of the dialogue, but then I added fifty percent more dialogue. I like to do that with actors.

When you begin to write, how much of a framework or design do you map out in advance? All of it. When you say, "how much" you got to know where you're starting, where you're going, and where you're going to wind up. See, theatrical comedy can't be written the way a novel is written. In a novel a guy sits downs and says, "I would like to tell you the story about myself. My name is David Copperfield, et cetera, et cetera," and you start to tell the story, hoping it will be interesting.

In writing for the theater it's not the story but the theatrical effect. How can I tell this story so that it will be *funny* and *exciting*? I won't start writing until I know where I can get a few big, strong theatrical effects. In that I include laughs, excitement, noise, whatever. I know a lot of guys start: page one, act one, scene one. They begin, hoping something funny will come up. No! I don't do it that way.

You might start on the second act in the last scene.
I may work on the middle of the first page, too. I
want to know where I'm going. I say, "This could
play funny because I could do so forth and so forth."
Sometimes one amusing line or thought will lead
me into a whole scene. I look for *highs* before I start
writing or rewriting. Sometimes one moment in the
scene is worth doing the whole scene for. If you start
the scene and you haven't got *highs,* the moment
may never hit. It's like traveling on a flat and never
climbing a mountain.
**To what extent can you predict the audience's
reaction to funny dialogue you've written?**
I can only go by the fact that they usually laugh
at what I laugh at. That's the only thing I can do.
What percentage of the time are you right?
By the time I open in New York, if I've got a hit,
I've been right all the time.
**Suppose in the tryouts the audience doesn't laugh.
Are there certain yardsticks you use to analyze why
they didn't respond?**
First thing, if it was played correctly, I don't
blame the audience. One of the deadliest things a
writer can do is say, "That's funny. It was a rotten
audience!" That's the *bum* idea. The audience is part
of your show. Sometimes there's a fire in the theater;
that may spoil a scene. But the audience is a group of
people, and if you blame them you're dead. Sometimes I've changed a reading—
By an actor?
Yes, or re-form the line a little bit because it was
too fast for the audience or too slow. Usually it's too
slow because the audience beats you to it or there
had been some disturbance—somebody walked

across the stage at the wrong time. Usually I go quickly to the line itself, and I say to myself, "I better get something else."

Naturally, by the time you open on Broadway the show is polished and ready, but I'm curious about the tryouts. Certainly everything you've written doesn't always get one hundred percent reaction.

No; but the hits have been funny from the start—first readings. There's a picture [*pointing to photograph on wall*] of myself, Cy Feuer the producer, and Frank Loesser at *How to Succeed*. We look pretty sad there. It's the very first reading, when nobody knew what was funny and what wasn't. We never got a laugh in the whole first reading. Usually you get laughs from the actors. There was nothing there. But I knew it was right somehow, and the first night in Philadelphia was a smash. Everything went. I was too long here and there. Some things were wrong, but nothing lay there. They don't generally lay with me. I know how to make them laugh—sometimes a wrong laugh.

A wrong laugh?

A laugh that distracts from something, changes a character, makes you dislike a guy, or tips something off that shouldn't be tipped off. That's editorial judgment.

Suppose the reaction to a line is small in a place you want a big laugh. Do you replace the line?

Depends on what I need. If the audience is smart and elegant and I like the line, I keep it. I got a couple of lines that just get smiles in some of my things, but they're right. They make good points; people remember them. The lines have value. When I need a big laugh, technically speaking—let's say at the blackout of a scene or a curtain because it is going to

take fifteen seconds to make the change for the next scene—I need something to carry the audience over that darkness in the theater. I need laughter or applause. Then I go for the "belly."
Is that where "technique" enters?
It's just experience, recognition. I know the kind of rhythm that'll probably work out a big laugh.
Rhythm?
The kind of a beat, the lead-up to a line. See, I think it's almost like an explosion. The longer you delay the audience from laughing at certain spots, the bigger the explosion will be—if you do it properly. When I work with an actor I'll say, "If you just delayed that by two beats"—there I use musical terms, two beats—"it'll be dynamite; or if you don't wait, it'll be dynamite. Either way." I kind of know that instinctively. That's like music. I never knew a good comedy writer who didn't have music in him.
How much of the laugh from a line depends on the actor's interpretation?
All of it, if he does it right. I'll say to an actor very frequently, "Don't help it!" One of the most difficult things to do is to read a line straight, as you wrote it, without helping it. If an actor tries to delay the punch line to help me, I say, "No; I punctuated it exactly the way I want it read. I don't want a pause before the snapper." Lots of times they argue with me. George Abbott told an actor who had lost a laugh he'd been getting for weeks—and this is a famous line—"Just say it!" That's the hardest thing to do— *just to say it.* The way the actor helps is to say the line the way you wrote it.
Chaplin once said, "If what you're doing is funny, you don't have to be funny doing it."
Charlie said that to me once. That's Bible to me. I

use it with every show. Actors are given a funny situation, and instead of playing it deadly *straight* they try to help it, try to be silly, funny. No! No!

After the lines have been written and the actors chosen, how much of the end result is the director responsible for?

The author is responsible for all of it; the director is responsible for all of it; and the actors are responsible for all of it. As a director, I consider myself one of the actors. The *first* director was probably an actor. I imagine some time in the Greek theater they said to a fellow, "Hey, Demetrius, you're not in this scene. Go out and see if we're loud enough; see if we're standing in front of each other; see if we make sense." So although I'm not on stage, I'm there to help *them* find the way to play it. I think of funny ways to do lines, and I give that to them. But they have to do it. The pain of the director on opening night is tremendous. I'm helpless.

I was the coauthor of *Guys and Dolls,* and George Kaufman directed that and he contributed so much. Now maybe another director can contribute more to my work than I can, but until I meet somebody better than I am as a comedy director, I don't believe it.

Y. A. Tittle and Dale Shofner* came to see Bobby Morse in *How to Succeed,* and they said to me: "Does he do that every night?" They were fascinated that the movements were the same every night—that we had it organized. They thought an actor walked around the stage the way he felt like it. We showed them that our moves, especially in the musical

---

*Former football heroes of the New York Giants.

theater, had even more precision than a football play. In the dressing room with Bobby Morse, Tittle showed him how he released the ball when Shofner made a move with his hips. We cut it even finer than that because the stage area is so small and there are actors constantly moving and crossing each other. **Then the job of a director is similar to that of a football coach?**

Yeah. It's choreographing the move, the cadence, the beat, pointing out where the line should come in and where the actor should let it go. I'm in back of the theater all the time, using body English. I say, "Let it go now, Murray; let it go!" It's like throwing that pass.

This ability to guide actors, to show them when to "throw the line"—how did you learn that?

Well, I learned more about my trade as a performer than I did as a writer. I know many writers who can't direct their own stuff. It also has to do with something else that isn't comedy talent. It's the ability to communicate. Some guys can't communicate with actors. It's like being a good father. The actors have to trust you. You've got to understand them. You've got to be firm and yet permissive. You've got to know each individual actor. If there are forty actors in the company, I have to know forty different ways to handle each one. Dictatorial directors, the ones who shout and holler and scream, sometimes get results, but generally they do very badly.

Is it important to write a play or musical that the audience can identify with?

It's always important, but who's to tell what they identify with? *How to Succeed* was about men

in business. There were practically no girls in the
show, yet women loved it as much as men. They
laughed at it because of their husbands' problems.
Obviously, to be successful a play must have something in it that people identify with, but you'll never
know in advance, because they identify with the
darndest things.

**How much do the times we live in dictate the kind of
play or musical that's written?**

As much as the times we live in dictate the kind
of guy you are. If you rebel against the times, you
write a certain kind of thing. If you're a slave to your
times, you write another kind of thing. The guys
who miss are the guys that sit down and say, "Look
here's what they want now. I'm gonna give it to
them." That you can never do.

Then it's a question of doing what you believe in?

The guys who put nudity in a show when they
don't like it themselves, figuring it's box office,
always blow it. If you try to match the times you'll
go mad. You'll never guess what the audience
wants. You can only know what *you* want. I'm
talking about professionals—sensible people with
some talent.

**You wrote the screenplay for *Solid Gold Cadillac*.
What specific problems are there in transforming a
stage comedy into a funny motion picture?**

In this particular case, I had the difficult
problem of taking a play that was written for Jose-
phine Hull, who was seventy-five, and making it a
love story for Judy Holliday, who was in her thirties.
And I solved it. It was a tremendous transformation,
but it came out rather delightful.

I had to write new scenes, new characters,
because it was a different girl; it was a love story

now. I went over the play a couple of times, and the big moments stuck in my head, and I worked towards them. I used them all. I don't think I left out a laugh that was in the play.

Then you have what is called "opening it up for the screen." You can't stay on one set. You can't stay indoors all the time. You have to blow it up. If you don't, you're not *using* film. You have to do things you couldn't show on the stage.

How important is financial security to a comedy writer's output?

That's a big point I've always debated. There are people who talk about subsidies for writers and artists. Some people say, "If a writer doesn't have the drive of needing money, he'll stop writing!" Incentive! Others say, "If he's taken care of financially, then he can face the real anxieties within himself, about being a creative artist!" I don't know what money has to do with it. Cole Porter and I did two shows together. He inherited a million dollars when he was eighteen, another two million when he was twenty-one. By the time he was thirty he was worth about ten million. By the time he died he had many millions. With all that money, Cole was the hardest-working man I ever worked with. He wrote day and night and long into the night, so the money didn't do it for him. Money wasn't the spur.

What is the spur?

Ah, that would be nice, if one knew, eh? Go back to what makes a guy write comedy. I say in a dreadfully simple way it's because that's what you do. It's like breathing. Maybe a lot of money would stop a guy. If I'd had a lot more money I would have turned down some of the things I did for dough. I didn't think I was doing it for the dough at the time. You always fool yourself. You say, "This would be a good thing," but you're really interested in the dough. Samuel Johnson said, "No man but a blockhead ever wrote except for money." I'm a professional. I was a much better writer the day I got two dollars for my first joke. I really *was* better the next day.

Then financial security does have some significance?

Financial security, no. There are two words there. Getting paid for something makes you better, because then you're a professional. When I wrote those panhandler jokes and loose jokes for Henny Youngman and I got paid, suddenly I sat down and I had more responsibility, and I gave my work more editorial thought. I didn't just dismiss it. I said, "A guy's gonna say this in front of people, and he's paying me for it; I'll give it a little more thought."

When you say "financial security," what do you mean? All the guys I know who've made a million dollars want to make two, so what's security? Security has to be inside of you, and it doesn't have much to do with money, if you have enough. You say, "I got my pile; I got enough." I had a friend who died worth sixty million dollars and each year he said, "If I get another million, I'm all right."

There seem to be a great number of comedy writers who are Jewish. Is there something in this ethnic group that seems to spawn artists with a bent for comedy?

It has to do with origin. Great comedy seems to have come out of Eastern Europe. People call it *Jewish* comedy. But it didn't come from the German Jews; it isn't true of the English Jews. But out of

Eastern Europe—Poland, Austria, Russia, the poverty areas—a kind of humor came from these people, came from their pain. And these people were very verbal. So the humor began to travel, and it was a very successful style of humor. Some fellows who were not Jewish at all picked a Jewish delivery because it was a successful way to work.

The comedy writers today who are Jewish then would be the sons and daughters of these people who immigrated to America.

Yeah; or grandsons. They heard that kind of humor. It was a kind of deprecating, put-down humor. Looking at Sholem Aleichem, you'll see the outpouring of it. He was the essence of Eastern European humor. Not specifically Jewish, because there are Jews all over the world who don't have that humor.

Is it possible to describe the requisites of becoming a comedy writer?

[*Laughing*] If I could say, "Pain you have to live with"—that might be one. It's a way of defending yourself. I've seen rich kids, kids who come from very happy homes, turn out pretty good comedy. I've seen poor kids do it. I used to think humor came from poverty, defeat. It's a darn quirk. I'm in constant communication with psychiatrists, analysts, who are interested in this whole subject of why people write comedy or what makes people laugh. One day I explained to one of them how you write a joke, how you deliver it by building up to a point and then explode it. And I finished, "They laugh!"

And he said to me, "Why don't they cry?" I was licked. I had no answer. There's a new translation of Freud's *Jokes and the Unconscious* by James Strachey. He goes into what is a joke? Why do people laugh? He thinks it gives them the feeling of superiority.

What other requisites are necessary for the would-be comedy writer?

For a guy to be a good comedy writer or a *better* comedy writer? Education will help him. Guys have done it without it, but I think they've lagged; it's kept them out of a great many fields. Education. Vocabulary. Without words, you're dead. Syntax!

For instance, I was an educated fellow when I was writing "Duffy's Tavern," and the show was full of malaprops, "mug talk." *Guys and Dolls* was full of "mug talk," but I could write that only because I knew the original. I know how to talk properly. I knew the proper use of a sentence. If you naturally talk that way, you're not going to be able to write it.

Comedy, which requires a twist of natural conversation, requires a knowledge of natural conversation, of real conversation. I try to tell kids, "If you've never read Shakespeare, you can't satirize the balcony scene from *Romeo and Juliet.*"

Then it's stretching the imagination, broadening the mind through reading and experience and—

By everything. A writer draws from himself. You see, there's no such thing as an original. A lot of people say this is an adaptation; that's an original. It's not true. An original is always based on something you know about, some uncle you had. So you're adapting something from your life; you're adapting from history, from something somebody told you. You're always adapting, and the more you *know* the more you can adopt—Maupassant, Boccaccio. You should have wide knowledge; that is a writer's tool.

Which may also lead to finding out the best area you're capable of working in.

I'm considered a satirist; I make fun of things. But I have something—maybe holds me back—I call it compassion. Max Beerbohm, the great critic, once said, "Satire should be based on a qualified love for the original." He wrote a book called *Zuleika Dobson,* which made fun of Oxford and Cambridge and the Knights of the Garter. He slaughtered them, kidded the pants off them, but basically he had an inner love for them. It wasn't hatred. What came out was very funny. Satire—comedy that's based on hatred—is seldom funny, seldom attractive.

The biggest compliment I could get was from *Time* magazine, when they reviewed *How to Succeed.* They said, "Burrows could have poured vitriol on big business; instead he painted a moustache on it." I've been in big business, and I thought it was silly. I got angry with it, but I didn't *hate* it. Hate can never produce humor. I guess that's why I couldn't write jokes about Hitler. I hated him, and to write comedy about him, hatred would be there and it wouldn't be funny.

Then you feel comedy comes out of love?

I think so—in an odd way. Defending yourself against the world, hitting back at your enemies.

. . . which is contrary to Freud's theory and those of others who believe that comedy comes from anger and hostility.

Yeah. Anger, hostility, defense, but not *hatred.* If it's hatred you can't make a joke anymore. The comedy writer attacks; he throws rocks; he uses a slingshot, bullets; but the reason it comes out comedy is because it's not full of hatred.

Bill
DANA

Bill Dana, son of Joseph and Dena Szathmary, was born on October 5, 1924, in Quincy, Massachusetts. After serving in the army as an infantryman, Bill Szathmary graduated from Emerson College with honors.

Then he changed the *e* in his mother's given name and took the name Dana when he began his show business career as a page at NBC with Gene Wood, a hometown buddy. Later, the two formed the comedy team of Dana and Wood.

After a successful tour of the country's chic supper clubs, the team split, and Dana became involved with the Imogene Coca and Martha Raye shows.

Dana then met and began writing for a young comedian named Don Adams, who often appeared on the old Steve Allen "Tonight Show." In time, Dana became a member of the Allen writing staff and subsequently went on to serve as chief scribe for "The Steve Lawrence and Eydie Gorme Show" as well as for "The Spike Jones Show," which he also produced.

After many appearances on other TV comedy

series, as Jose Jimenez, Bill finally starred in his own series, "The Bill Dana Show."

Dana, with his alter ego, Jose Jimenez, has recorded seven hit comedy albums, written a book, *My Name Jose Jimenez,* and inspired a cartoon series, "The Adventures of Uncle Jose."

Dana also has to his credit an Emmy Award-winning segment on "All in the Family," in which Sammy Davis visited. He is currently making appearances in film, on TV, and in America's leading nightclubs.

At the time of the interview Bill Dana was a bachelor living on top of a high hill in a nine-room home overlooking Hollywood's famed Sunset Strip. He referred to it as his "Mediterranean-type house"—no two rooms were on the same level.

Dana used three rooms for work. One was outside his bedroom; another was an office; and a third, filled with electronic equipment, used for this interview, was a small sitting room with a fireplace. All available wall space was filled with paintings and books.

Bill wore a white Jungle Jim sport shirt with green and black slacks and brown slippers.

Before the talk began, Dana provided a guided tour of the house, during which he joked about everything. He is highly sensitive and takes comedy quite seriously. He was relaxed and eagerly expressed his views.

After this interview took place, Bill Dana married, moved to Hawaii and was divorced. Once again now he lives in Hollywood.

You grew up in Quincy, Massachusetts, and—

I was *born* in Quincy, Massachusetts, and I stayed there for many years, but until this date, I've never *grown up.* That's my problem. That's what I'm working on now.

Quincy is a quiet New England town. You finished school and then went on to college—all the so-called normal elements of an average person's upbringing. What do you feel were the abnormal or unusual aspects of your environment that led you to become a comedy writer?

It's very hard to answer that. At Quincy High School I did kibbitz around. In the school annual it said, "Class Comedian, Class Actor." I was a very, very *introverted* guy, and I guess perhaps I was overcompensating. I was a skinny little kid—this story has been told over and over again; I believe it's a pattern: the depression baby, being Jewish and having those hang-ups. It sends you in a direction. You have to be kind of fast on your tongue, to get out of fights and so forth.

I came from a music-oriented family. My father was in the real estate business—when he was working. He had nothing to do with show business, but he had brothers who were musicians, violinists. My oldest brother, Irving, was music director of "Get Smart." My brother Sid is a violinist with the Indianapolis Symphony. My brother Arthur is a professor of philosophy at Princeton and sort of an authority on art and music. So you see, I've been involved with *rhythm,* which is very much, as you know, a part of comedy.

What do you think were the psychological or emotional reasons that led you into comedy?

As far back as I can remember, I always looked at things in a tangential way—I always twisted things around—and that's pretty much what comedy is. Fortunately, it didn't come out in a smart-alecky way. My insecurities were so great as a kid that when I would think of something "clever," I would always attribute it to someone else. "Do you know what I heard?" Then I would say something I had thought of. I didn't want it to be mine in case people didn't laugh at it or they put it down. It's only in the past several years I have overcompensated. Now I'm terribly conceited about my prowess as a comedy writer.

In a *TV Guide* interview you said that you "grew up in the depression and that nothing breeds humor better than adversity." Are poverty and hardship the only ingredients for seeing the funny side of life?

I don't think so. My God, the Kennedy family have great wit. They are not *necessary* ingredients. I remember when the bill collector was knocking on the door and we had the curtains pulled down and the voice, muffled through the door, would say, "We know you're in there!"

And somebody in the family would say, "We know we're in here, too!" and we would giggle about it.

One hears that many jokes come from prisons and the concentration camps. A lot of Stalag 17 humor has come out of adversity. Personal insecurities or financial insecurities have kept me pretty much on the alert and have forced me to work more. I would never attribute a percentage of the amount of comedy that comes out of adversity, but I would certainly say that *some* comes out of it.

In that same article you said that "there's nothing like stepping out in front of an audience and getting that approval, that big wonderful moment of love." Were you saying that there is more satisfaction in performing than in writing?

In the erotic sense, there is. Oh, yes! There is a

difference in the satisfaction one gets from making love to a woman compared to the satisfaction one gets from finishing a painting.
Which is which?

When you perform and the people dig what you're doing, applause smothers you with love. There is great satisfaction, a unique satisfaction in performing, just as there is a unique destruction if things don't go right. I had to educate my own managers. I said to them, "I don't care what I do on that stage. When I come off, I'm like litmus paper. I react. Lie to me if you don't think I did a good job. In that moment, don't tell me *anything*—tell me something neutral." Everybody knows when they've dropped a bomb, and they know when they have done well.

Along with Jackie Gleason's Ralph Cramden, Jose Jimenez has become a classic comic character. How was he created?

Jose was born out of a joke. Don Hinkley and I used to write "The Steve Allen Show," and one of the departments we had was the Weekly Nutley Hinkley Buckley Report. We had four announcers strategically located, reporting in depth on whatever was happening in the United States. Out of this came Dayton Allen's "Why not?" Jose Jimenez came out of this, just before Thanksgiving 1959 on a Pre-Christmas Report, USA. I came up with a joke: Santa Claus says, "Ho, ho, ho." But if he were Latin, he would still say, "Ho, ho, ho," but if you saw it spelled you would see it with a J—Jo, jo, jo.

At the script meeting with Steve, Jules Green, Bill Harback, Nick Vanoff, Stan Burns, Herb Sergent, and all the writers, I was usually given the assignment to read and a lot of times to *sell* what we had. I was the *performer* on the writing staff.

Jimenez was born in Los Angeles, but back in New York across from the Hudson Theatre (where we first did the Allen show) there was a restaurant called the Oasis. There was a man who used to come and take orders for food who was Puerto Rican. He talked like dat. He said, "Wha yu guys wan? Wan coffee blac. . ." Once in a while I would walk in with a pad and say, "OK, anybody order from the Oasis."

The Allen staff knew I did this dialect. I did all the dialects. So in this meeting I'm talking about, Steve said, "Why don't you do it, Bill?" So it was an accident that I played the part of Jose Jimenez, as an instructor in a Santa Claus school. Jimenez is more sophisticated today. It's almost like Bill Dana just talking with a Latin accent.

Is it possible to break down and pinpoint Jose's specific comic characteristics?

A lot of people said that you laugh at Jose because he's bumbling and inept. I challenge that. They laugh at him because he is mouthing goddamn good jokes. I've done Jose Jimenez jokes in Scotch, German, Yiddish dialects. People are laughing at well-constructed jokes. I stole back a joke for the Jimenez character that Don Hinkley and I wrote for George Gobel. Jose was a rancher. "What is the name of your ranch?"

And Jose said, "The name of my ranch is the Bar Nine, Circle Z, Rocking O, Flying W, [pause] Lazy R, Crazy Nine, Bar Seven, [pause] Happy Two, Flying Nun, Lazy Six, Bar Eight Ranch."

"Do you have many cattle?"

Jose says, "Not many survived the branding. You talk about screaming cows. That was some barbecue we had. There was twelve acres of flaming flanken out there."

The thing about Jimenez—there was a certain acceptability, lovability, hugability. Stan Burns used to say, "Jose Jimenez is one of the few men I'd like to hug." That's a big plus. Jimenez is a Pollyanna character who wants to do well. His motives are always to do the best things. He's an assimilated American, therefore much more aware of what it is to be an American. An extension, perhaps, of *The Education of H*Y*M*A*N K*A*P*L*A*N.* Jimenez is not an original concept at all. Leo Rosten wrote *H*Y*M*A*N K*A*P*L*A*N* years and years ago.

Let's take one Jimenez routine, Jose, the astronaut. What was the step-by-step writing process?

Well, there are two Jose Jimenezes. One is the Walter Mitty Jimenez and one is the flesh-and-blood Jimenez. The Walter Mitty Jimenez was Jose, the astronaut; Jose, the skin diver; Jose, the submarine commander; this is the guy everybody knows is not what he pretends to be. On the Bill Dana show, Jose was a bellman. He had the problems of the hotel and guest—he was a flesh-and-blood character.

Let's get back to the astronaut routine.

OK. The astronaut didn't happen until a good *year* after Jose was born and had been accepted, and I had an album out which was a very big seller. I never got any money. It was on the Signature label which went bankrupt. Well, no use crying over spilt wax.

Anyway, Jose, the astronaut, came from a suggestion by Neil Simon when he was writing the Garry Moore show. Don Hinkley and I wrote the routine. It was an overnight success, because you had the dialect, the character going for you. The laughs came out of the comic character rather than the specific jokes. There are no big jokes in Jose, the astronaut, but one line was picked up and constantly repeated in advertising offices: "I plan to cry a lot!"

Jose worked under peril. Everybody empathizes with fear. It was Alan Shephard who, during the countdown for his first suborbital flight, had the record played over the loudspeakers at what was then Cape Canaveral. He was the one that really made Jose, the astronaut.

In a *New York Post* article by Sally Hammond you explained the difference between acting Jose and writing for Jose. You said, "The acting is easy but writing a weekly show is like infantry basic training." How can one aspect of creating be so difficult and the other phase so easy?

When I had my show, I found that there were two kinds of writers. One type was in trouble because of basic incompetence. There are people in our business making very healthy salaries who are complete incompetents. A lot of them started out in radio and in television that have a couple of credits, and they continue doing either twists on stuff that they wrote years ago or on stuff that somebody did last night. OK. That's the type writer that's incompetent.

There's another type that's incompetent, but he's a good writer; he's forced to be incompetent by time and pressure. "Hey, Harry, is Lou there? Get on the line; will you, guys? Listen, we're in trouble. We need a script; we only got three days. I know you're working on 'The Carol Burnett Show.' Remember the thing you did for Joey Bishop? All we need is a little twist on that thing."

So there's a producer who is forcing writers to prostitute themselves and the writers say, "OK." They may do it as a favor, or they may do it because there's a little hooker in them.

Hooker?

Whore! I know because I've done it. This is why you find a lot of stars of their own shows saying, "I don't know what the writers are doing around here. We did this when it all happened on the set!" Strangely enough a lot of times that is true. You get a basic premise to work around, and the characters know what they're supposed to say and do, and you let it happen. There have been writers who have taken bows for shows in which they wrote exactly three apostrophes and five semicolons in the script.

Writing a half-hour situation comedy and trying to keep it fresh, trying to stay away from stereotyped plots and trying to keep the thing honest in that space of time—that's what is like infantry basic training. On top of the commitment you have to have literary honesty. Then you have rehearsal, wardrobe, makeup. You've got personality problems to put up with.

Did you write each segment?

No, no! I did an awful lot of writing. Some scripts I wrote from page one, others with somebody else. It was the rewriting process that was tortuous.

Many writers doing a situation comedy series for TV collaborate with another writer. What is the value in that?

It's ping-pong. It's hard to ping unless somebody else pongs. It's good to bounce ideas off somebody. Some things I like to write in collaboration. I'm naturally gregarious. I like to be with people. A lot of things I like to write alone. The things I write alone are the things I feel have substance. I guess that's a matter of ego, because when you're finished polishing the gem, you can say, "Hey, that belongs to me!" You don't have to share it with anyone else.

When Steve Allen signed you as one of his writers,

you said that it was "the best acceleration course in comedy writing I could ever have." Did you mean then that to be a comedy writer you can only learn by experience?

I don't like to pontificate . . . What the hell! My opinion is that like actors and comedians you cannot *become* a comedy writer. You cannot *become* an actor; you cannot *become* a comic. You are *born* a comic, and you can become better at it by experience, by aid, by counsel.

If somebody doesn't *think* funny, nobody in the world is going to teach him how to think funny. You just can't do it. It's not in human nature. You have to have the blade. You can hone the edge and make it sharp. If you don't have a sense of humor or a sense of acting or a sense of dramatics, ain't nobody going to teach you how to do it. For a short while I taught an extension course at UCLA, and that's the first thing I told them. "There are eighty or ninety people in this class. If there is one comedy writer here, I would be very much surprised." There wasn't one! There were two or three that had some notion what was funny, and that's about it.

What were some specific techniques you learned while serving your "apprenticeship" with Steve Allen?

I learned something that is good and also bad— formulization. I learned how to use a formula quickly and how to disguise it. I can do—for the layman—the same joke five different ways and he won't know it's the same joke.

What is a "formula"?

Well, people say there are seven basic jokes— there are as many basic jokes as there are formulas that are created. We talked about the "Bar Nine,

Circle Z, Rocking O" joke. You can make that into a formula. It's just something that has a surprise answer.

Like the "long license plate number" joke?

Yeah. That happens to be a joke I wrote for the warm-up of the Imogene Coca show. It took the form of an announcement. "Anybody in the audience with a New York license plate BL 7446745893062314-5098725, will you kindly move it. Your license plate is blocking traffic." That joke can be done in many ways.

You said formulization could be good and bad.

Formulization can be good because you need it to survive in television. It's bad because after a while it might become too easy. I know myself that I have done the same thing over and over again—too many times. Once in a while you come up with a new one. I was extremely proud of one I came up with for a Jackie Gleason show. It had to do with Jimenez being a member of the Miami Dolphins. My number was 305.

Gleason said, "Jose, what would you say was your most thrilling experience?"

"My most prettiest experience in football happened during a football game!"

"What happened?"

"The ball came, it got kicked to me and I grabbed the ball and started to run down the field and I ran five yards and they tried to stop me and they couldn't stop me and they took out pistols; they shot at me and they still couldn't stop me and I kept running and they shot me with rifles and they couldn't stop me—"

"Wait a minute!" Gleason said.

"And then they brought the cannon out on the

field and they shot me with the cannon and then the airplanes came down with machine guns and they didn't stop me and finally I made a touchdown."

"Wait a second," Gleason said. "How can you stand here in front of all these people and say something that is obviously a lie. Anybody who was in the stadium that day could prove that that was a lie."

And Jose said, "There were no survivors."

Did you learn more writing for Don Adams than you did working for Steve Allen?

No, not necessarily. Don was the first person I ever wrote for. Don had this character which was really an impression of William Powell. One of my great kvellings* is that I brought Don out here and put him on my show as the detective, and the "Get Smart" thing happened. I wrote all the earlier routines for Don. The baseball umpire school, the football coach. My salary, by the way, was ten percent of his salary, and at that time he was making about 150 bucks a week.

That's very important in the development of a young comedian. Having a comedy writer with whom he has a great rapport, someone who not only writes funny lines but can also guide and nurture him.

I first met Don in 1953. Another routine I did was the defense attorney. "Your honor, ladies and gentlemen of the jury, for the past twenty minutes I sat by while the prosecuting attorney stood up here making a complete ass of himself. Now it's my turn!" This marriage you're talking about was very, very important in my career. It was the beginning of a series of accidents in which I became a comedy writer. Mace Neufeld got Don and me together.

---

*Jewish word for proud feelings.

Writers, in discussing comedy theory, often refer to the "willing suspension of disbelief." What exactly does that mean?

When people laugh, it's a relief. They want to forget their working day, their troubles. So if they have to let themselves think that a huge boulder can fall from a mountain and land on the animal that's chasing the road runner and that he will come out in the shape of a long strip of celluloid and then out into something else—there are children and child adults who laugh at that. Anybody who is intelligent knows that Jack Benny is not a frugal man. He's very generous. You have to believe that he's a penny-pincher in order to laugh at him.

It's what I call the Lili syndrome. You know the motion picture *Lili*? Leslie Caron played it. It's a story about a puppeteer. Children and even adults come and talk to a puppet as though it had a life of its own. There's no way a child or a child adult can enjoy that moment if they're going to say, "This is a piece of cloth over somebody's fist." That is the willingness to suspend disbelief.

Someone taking a course in creative writing or journalism or playwriting can learn the basic methods and techniques. Are there also rules for creating jokes?

I could give you the mathematics of some jokes. I could give you the anatomy of a specific joke. We touched on that when we talked about formulization. I don't like it, because you're leaving yourself open to quite a bit of sterility. I don't like to have rules. I can call upon a repertoire of already constructed jokes or skeletons I know exist, and I could put different flesh on.

Like what?

The "would you believe" joke I wrote in 1954 is one of those jokes that is a formula. I'll give you the original. The British in India. Don Adams as Leftenant Favershim confronting Mohammed Sidney Kahn. Adams as Favershim: "Not so fast. Sahib Kahn, you may think you've got me, but I've got you surrounded by the entire Mounted Seventeenth Bengal Lancers!"

The Kahn says, "I don't believe that!"

"Would you believe the *First* Bengal Lancers!"

"No!"

"How about Gunga Din on a donkey?"

That formula has been driven into the ground. We used it extensively on the Dana show, and Don took it to his own show. The "would you believe" has become a part of the American colloquial language.

Here's another example of the formula joke. On "The Steve Allen Show" we had a routine called the Question Man. It was one of the most gratifying things to learn—Peter Lawford told me—that this was one of President Kennedy's favorite jokes. The premise of the Question Man was that today everybody knows all the answers. There are more answers then there are questions. Well, the answer was: "Chicken Teriyaki."

And the question was: "Give me the name of the oldest kamikaze pilot."

In the book *Harold Lloyd's World of Comedy*, Lloyd said, "Every comedian has to be a scholar of comedy so that he can know just what he is doing." Is being a scholar of comedy also a requirement for a comedy writer?

That requisite would be stronger for the comedy writer than the comedian, because in the beginning is the *word*. The comedian shows up on the set and someone has to hand him a piece of paper with words on it.

How would a comedy writer go about becoming a "scholar of comedy"? What would he look for? What would he study? What would he try to understand?

In my formative days I tried not to be a scholar of comedy. Until this day I do not have a joke file. I wanted everything that came out of my head or mouth to be fresh and new. That cross-index file that Berle has is a fantastic thing, but it leads you down treacherous paths. It gives you saneness. I like to change with the times. I'm an observer of the passing scene. If I see something that strikes me funny, I make a note of it. A lot of times, things I think can be amplified into a screenplay will end up as a paragraph or one line in something I'll write.

Is there any logical reason why the majority of comedy writers are Jewish?

It goes back to adversity. A lot of them came from the Lower East Side or from another geographical approximation of it. I think my Jewishness is involved in whatever I do. I love the Irish whimsy. I think Bobby Ball is one of the funniest men alive. He's sort of an Irish Lenny Bruce. He was a depression baby. We often talk about the Irish, the Jew, the Italian—there's wit in all of these groups.

Members of minority—

Yeah, Negros certainly. Comedy came out of the fact that they had to laugh their way through, being persecuted all these years.

Ernest Hemingway once said, "Often the best part of a novel is left in bed." Does sex affect your creative output?

Yes, very much so. In the first place, the hand-writing gets very shaky. . . spill ink and everything.

Seriously. Does sex have a debilitating or enervating effect on your creative energy?

No; I've made some of my best jokes coupled with ladies. I call them couplets.

What about liquor? Do spirits in any form help stimulate the creative process?

Ummm, no. I find sometimes a couple of belts help to relax, but I like to do it at the end of a working day. If you are on an assignment, it's a little bit dangerous to get too relaxed. I love booze, by the way.

Suppose you have a deadline to make on a TV script and you can't come up with a satisfactory idea because the creative juices aren't flowing. What do you do to get yourself in the proper frame of mind?

Well, I have always in the freezer compartment some creative juices. I never had that problem. I've never had that "coming up dry" cliché feeling. I started out with tremendous insecurity and inferiority feelings. Now I have an inordinate respect for myself as a comedy writer.

Do you have any specific work habits you adhere to?

No; I find that if I am involved with a show and if the show is in production, I like to work in an office, be near to what's happening. I think that's important.

Is there any difference in your attitude toward life as you sit here unconcerned about rent or food money compared to the days when you were scratching for a buck?

No cockroaches in the corner! Well, the difference is twofold. I love the creature comforts, and I'm very grateful that I have the criterion of poverty to measure by. When I reach into my pocket and feel a few bucks, I really dig it. I hope I always do. That's in the plus column. In the minus column, there's a certain mystique, a certain thrill, a certain mystery for every telephone call, every knock on the door in those days, because that might be the break. Those were great feelings when I was a page with Gene Wood in 1950, '51, and early '52.

I was making thirty-five dollars a week, and everybody knows I make twice that now. There were things that were fun then that I don't have today. You have to pay the piper, as they say. You have to give up something to get something in addition. I enjoy what I have, and sometimes I feel guilty for it. **In the beginning were you influenced by any particular writers?**

I volunteer Mark Twain as being the greatest humorist, wit, comedian, or whatever you want to call him, in the history of the world. God, the way he saw things! He just tore the facade off religion and humanity. You must read Twain's *Letters from the Earth*—it's just fantastic. Bill Cosby, Lenny Bruce—everything they did—it's all there, almost word for word.

Is there any advice you can offer someone who wants to be a comedy writer?

Yeah. Ask yourself, "Are you a comedy writer?" And if the answer is, "Yes!" then ask yourself, "Are you willing to become a better comedy writer?" How you get an audience, an ear or an eye for your material—that's an enigmatic problem. It's a goddamn shame it has to depend so much on luck.

When I was head writer, Steve Allen gave an open invitation for everybody to send in material, and I had to go through that stuff. Out of every thousand pages, if you could find one funny sentence it was a miracle. That's why comedy is the

uranium of show business. There's just so little of it
of real value. And it's going to stay that way a long
time. Just as a diamond needs to be under tremendous pressure over millions of years in the ground,
a similar process has to happen to create a comedian or a comedy writer, and it just doesn't happen
that often.

The
MIDDLE

I n the last ten years the open prejudice toward
women writing comedy has begun to disappear.
Back in the days of radio, having females turn out
grist for the jester's mill was practically unheard of.
Alyce Walker was a pioneer in that era. She wrote
for Eddie Cantor, Al Jolson, Martha Raye, and
others, starting in 1937. Today she conducts an
interview show in Palm Springs on station KWXY.

There are many gifted females who earn their
bread by the quip:

Lucille Kallen, one of the first to break through
on TV, cut her comedy teeth on "The Sid Caesar
Show."

Lila Garrett has two Emmys, one as writer of the
year, the other for a special of the year. Miss Garrett
has the distinction of being the only female producer in situation comedy.

Iris Rainer is a key member of the staff on the
Cher show.

Sandra Harmon wrote "The Dick Cavett Show"
for four years, the first all-female comedy show, and
a recent novel, *A Girl Like Me.*

Gail Parent, with her partner Kenny Solms, has written for Steve Allen and Carol Burnett as well as writing the Broadway show *Lorelei*. Her novel, *Sheila Levine Is Dead and Living in New York,* was a runaway best-seller and a major motion picture.

Treva Silverman has a long list of comedy credits, including "Room 222," "That Girl," and "The Mary Tyler Moore Show," in addition to her efforts on behalf of Dean Martin and Bill Cosby.

Elaine May helped create the classic comedy routines she performed for years with Mike Nichols. She has since adapted *A New Leaf* for the screen and has written and directed the motion picture *Mikey and Nickey*.

Renee Taylor (with her husband, Joe Balogna) created and wrote several episodes for the television comedy series "Calucci's Dept." Their hilarious motion pictures, *Lovers and Other Strangers* and *Made for Each Other*, have received high critical praise.

These are just a few of the talented women who have contributed to tickling America's funnybone. One woman, however, is considered to have started the trend. Many women don't like to talk about their age, so it would be indelicate to call Selma Diamond the grand old lady of comedy. But she was the first of the females to become famous whipping up funnies for the top comedy shows.

Selma
DIAMOND

Selma Diamond was born and grew up in Brooklyn. Although she will not divulge her age, she
candidly admits that she is unmarried and does not
lack for dates.

Miss Diamond began her writing career with
Groucho Marx. She subsequently worked for
Jimmy Durante, Tallulah Bankhead, Milton Berle,
Sid Caesar, and Perry Como.

After her first television appearance with Jack
Paar, *Look* magazine dubbed her "the Corduroy
Voice," while *Newsweek* referred to the "vocal cords
that got lodged away up in her sinuses." She has
since demonstrated her scintillating wit on the Merv
Griffin, Mike Douglas, and Joan Rivers shows. She
also has appeared on stage in *Bye, Bye Birdie* with
Andy Williams and Tom Poston and *Don't Drink the
Water* with Sam Levene.

Miss Diamond is currently preparing a book of
observations.

Selma Diamond dwells in a very simply decorated apartment in a very luxurious building on New
York's fashionable Sutton Place.

For our talk, she wore a blue-and-white-striped jersey, blue slacks, orange sandals, and a gold, diamond-studded bracelet watch. She is very much at ease, laughing often during the interview while smoking cigarettes and drinking soda pop. Selma Diamond is an ingenuous, straightforward woman who conveys her views openly and without pretense.

Miss Diamond's comedic skills are well illustrated by this anecdote which she cleverly worked into our conversation:

"I returned to my old neighborhood after writing comedy in Hollywood for nine years, and I dropped into Landsman's candy store wearing my classy new clothes. I waited for Landsman to say something, and finally I said, 'You know where I've been?'

"He looked at me for a second and said, 'You been goin' across the street?' "

Your first professional writing job was with Groucho Marx. Had you written for any other comedians before that?

No. I didn't even think of myself as a comedy writer. I wanted to write something, and I just decided it right then—it's show business. I'm like that.

What did you do before that?

I used to sell little things to augment my very meager allowance. The *Daily News* had "How He Proposed" as a feature. I used to write it for five or ten dollars. They had "Most Embarrassing Moments." and I used to make up those, too.

How did the job with Groucho come about?

I went to Hollywood, walked into *Variety,* and I

said to Jack Hellman, "Put it in the paper that I'm here."

He said, "Who are you?"

I said, "What difference does it make? I would like to be a comedy writer." So he sent me to see a producer. I showed him some material, and he ignored it. He wasn't too impressed with me or the material. I don't know if he even read it.

He said, "No, we have plenty of people." Then I remembered that I had once met someone from the William Morris Agency—this was when I was still going to school, and I had shown him something that I had written—who said if I ever came to the Coast I should look him up. So I did, and he sent me to the *same* producer and I got a job.

Did you take any writing courses in school?

No, I didn't take one. They have courses, but I took nothing. I wasn't a scholar, I would say.

Arnold Auerbach, in his book *Funny Men Don't Laugh,* described his apprenticeship with a famous gag writer. Auerbach's job at the beginning was to file jokes under specific categories. How did you learn the craft of comedy writing?

I think you learn by doing it. I only learned by doing. I just kept writing and writing and I'm still writing.

You can't be sure of anything. I do know in certain sections of the country if you say "slob" or "Green Bay Packers" they're going to laugh.

I learned that if it's based on truth, then you just think funny. An actor has a one-eyed cat who jumped out of a sixth-floor hotel room to commit suicide. That's funny! I see the cat is in a cast. Why did the cat jump? She was probably tired of being on the road, locked up in a hotel room. This probably was her first attempt, because if it was her ninth she'd be dead. That's what humor is.

You spent a number of years working with Goodman Ace. In what way did Ace influence you and the development of your talent?

His influence was to make me show up on time. I guess you would call him a master. I learned from him the way I learned from everybody else. If I wrote something that worked I learned. I don't know any other way.

Were there any specific techniques you learned?

I don't think there's a specific technique. You write funny; that's all. I don't know what you mean by techniques. You mean you approach something in a specific way? I know if you're writing a sketch, just like a play or a monologue, it's got to have a beginning, a middle, and an end. And the audience has got to be interested in it, and they've got to think it's funny.

You are particularly skilled in creating what is known as the one-line gag.

No; I write those, but I also write sketches. I got that reputation because I've done so many variety shows for so many comedians. But working for Sid Caesar certainly did not mean one-line jokes.

What exactly are the components of a one-line joke?

It might be something topical. It's got to be about something the audience can identify with, what they read about in the paper that morning or the weather.

Common denominator subjects.

Yes, yes. It's like sex; humor is the great leveler. If you're enjoying it you're equal. You're identifying.

Many writers follow the rule to use no more than two

straight or unfunny lines to get the gag line. Is that a basic technique?

Anybody that is using two *unfunny* lines can't think of two funny lines. I would no more approach something by first saying, "Let me think of something unfunny"—I try and think of something *funny*. Sometimes I *build* to a funny line.

You told a joke about the one-eyed cat that jumped out of a sixth-floor hotel room before you got to the punch line. You had to set up the joke. Do you consider that all one sentence?

That depends on the delivery of the performer. Some performers do it in one sentence. It depends on their timing, whether they do *verbal* takes. When you write for a comedian you are aware of the way he works. You hear his sound, his rhythm, and you write with that sound in mind.

You mentioned words that sound funny—"Green Bay Packers," "slob" . . .

Those are words you use in a joke. It's like slang. Like "smoking bananas." Last year bananas didn't mean anything. Today you say, "I have a teen-ager home so I can't keep bananas in the house." Because everybody's talking about the kids. Again that's recognition. People have to identify.

Then a writer must be extremely aware of what's going on.

Absolutely. *More* than that. I've worked with comedians and writers who when you come up with a topical or political joke they say, "The audience wouldn't get it!" My answer was, "*You* don't get it!" There are a lot of comedians who turn to the columns and that's it. They never look at the front page. Whereas the man in the street— Look at the circulation the *News* and the *Times* have. You pass a newspaper stand; it's stacked high with morning papers, magazines. Now somebody's reading them. I'm constantly reading magazines, newspapers, just to keep up with people, because poeple are smarter than anybody. I've discovered that.

Is it possible to take a joke written for Milton Berle and tailor it to fit Perry Como?

Of course. If it's a good joke, a good comedian can tell it. You just have to do it in his style.

Could you give me an example?

I'd rather not. I may never work again. They'd all recognize the joke. It's done. Everybody does it. I don't keep a file in this house. Once I've finished a show, I don't keep the scripts. The good jokes you remember, and the bad ones you want to forget. I can't keep a lot of junk around the house.

You said before that when you are working for a comedian you have to hear the sound of his voice, how he delivers. Is it also necessary to understand how he thinks, what his philosophy is?

I don't think when a comedian goes out to work he reveals his *real* self or his *philosophy*. He's playing a part. Bob Hope stands up there and delivers jokes like Peck's Bad Boy. He's *far* from that. He's a very intelligent, rich man. When I or somebody like me goes on a talk show, we reveal ourselves, but performers don't. They work on that image they have. Milton Berle projects that brashness. Milton is a real gentleman. It's been years since I've worked for him, yet if I go out to dinner with him and his lovely wife, he will remember what I smoke, what I drink. He's not that brash offstage. He has many serious thoughts.

So the comedian's personal beliefs, his personal likes and dislikes are not important when it comes to writing comedy for him?

They're only important if they relate to what the audience is thinking. If there's a comedian who goes around sticking knives in people—which isn't nice—or he wants to shoot somebody, he will not reveal this to his audience. He reveals what the audience has accepted as his image.

What about the new comedian who hasn't yet been accepted by the vast majority of people? Can a comedy writer help him find his image?

Yes. If a comedian and a writer get together they can develop something. A good writer can watch the comedian's mannerisms, his face, look at his appearance, the way he dresses, and find something that he can blow up and develop into an image.

Can you write for a comedian even though you personally don't think he's funny?

I have! But I know what makes him funny, and I can write that. He may not be the kind of guy I might laugh at, but I know why the audience is laughing at him. And besides, you write to order.

Most of the comedians you have written for have been men. Is it just as easy to write a joke from a man's point of view, even though you're a woman?

Let's get that straight. I don't write from a man's point of view. Sex doesn't come into that at all. A woman playwright, she's writing parts for men and women. I think being a woman has given me a slight edge. I become aware of new fashions and trends before the fellows do. There have been many occasions when I'd come up with jokes that the comedian and the writers backed away from because they didn't know what I was talking about. So you get down on your knees and you say, "Please try it!" And then they're surprised when it works. I think that has definitely given me an edge.

Also, women are more sensitive. I have more

things that I don't write about because I'm a woman.
I can't write a joke about physical disability. I'm
repelled when I see a comedian stuttering or limp-
ing. I don't know whether I'm sensitive about that
because I'm a woman or because I'm me.

It also comes under the heading of taste.

I'm glad you brought that up. That is the most
important thing. I wouldn't write chauvinistic
jokes—jokes where the character is speaking English incorrectly because he's a foreigner. The stingy
Scotsman, the drunk Irishman—ethnic jokes. Now I
wish I had written *Fiddler on the Roof,* because the
person who wrote all those stories was writing the
truth.

**You don't like the put-down joke in which a member
of a minority group is made to look foolish or stupid.**

Absolutely. I've seen old-time comedies where
the Irishman is drunk and fighting all the time; the
Chinese laundryman has a long braid and the kids
are running after him; the man with the derby runs
the pawnshop. We're living in an era today where
this type of thing doesn't exist, and we haven't had
that kind of thing since immigration at the turn of
the century. It's not true that all the Irish drink and
fight. All blacks don't carry razors. Stereotypes,
like Stepin Fetchit. I am repelled by that. I think that
keeps us back as a culture. It's just bad taste, and I
can't stand it.

**As a female, were there any particular problems
you had to overcome to become a comedy writer?**

Yes. It's like being Red China. I'm there; they
just won't accept me. That's the hostility that men
and women have. It's a natural thing. When I first
started, I was very young and I couldn't understand
it. Then I noticed that men working with each other

are hostile. So I don't think it's because I was a
woman; I think it's because I was another writer.
Men aren't that nice to each other; you should know
that.

Did you feel antagonism from the male writers?

I always felt there was hostility between the
head writer and the other writers. They all felt they
should be the head writer. I was working on a
show—I was now moving up there—and a beginner
came on the show and the other writers wouldn't
even have lunch with him. I don't have that problem.
I'm not afraid if someone sees me sitting with somebody. So I used to go to lunch with the new guy. One
of the fellows on the show said, "You're sitting in the
Derby with him, and people are going to say you and
he are in the same class as writers." See, the caste
system I just don't dig at all.

Why are there so few female comedy writers?

I really don't know. Why are there so few female
wives?

**Some psychologists feel that comedy writers are
rebels against their backgrounds. Do you think that
was the psychological motivation for you to become
a writer?**

I don't go with psychological motivation for
anything. You do something because you want to. I
was not a funny kid. In school, I was not the comedian of the class. I never put on a funny hat. I still
don't. I'm just a human being who thinks funny. I
also have my serious moments.

**Have you ever tried to analyze what made you
decide to write comedy?**

What makes you decide to do anything? You've
got to start making a living. I chose comedy writing
because it's something I can do. Sometimes when I

get depressed because a job only lasts two or three days, I say to myself, "What the heck am I doing this for?" Then I think about something else I could be doing and I get scared stiff and I'm glad I'm a comedy writer.

Goodman Ace, in his *Book of Little Knowledge,* **says of your first meeting, "Miss Diamond displayed all the symptoms peculiar to a talented mass-medium comedy writer." Is it possible to define "mass-medium comedy writer"?**

Yes. What I think Goody meant was I could relate to the masses. What you identify with you can write funny. Being aware, as I said before—reading, writing. I've heard great things on a bus, many funny things in restaurants that have started me thinking. It all comes from people, and the people will laugh if they recognize what the comedian is talking about.

Then a writer has to be somewhat of a mass psychologist?

I can't use words like *psychologist* or *analyst.* I'd rather use the word aware of what's going on. I've got to be aware that there are pool parlors. You've got to be aware that students are rioting, that there are political conventions. You've got to know what's going on, and you've got to be part of it. That goes for all types of writers. You can't just limit yourself to sitting in the Brown Derby or Danny's Hideaway. You must remember that there are people eating at Horn & Hardart's, and there are people who are not eating at all.

Comedians are often described as highly neurotic egomaniacs who are insecure and frightened. Doesn't that make your job practically impossible?

Any successful person is nervous. As far as

being a writer, who isn't? I'm sure the manager of
the A&P does things that other people would think
are neurotic. Comedians might be called neurotic
because they make a lot of money and then the bills
come in and they need more. We're all neurotic. A
successful man is called more neurotic because he's
rubbing more people the wrong way. The head of a
chain of restaurants is just as nervous. It's responsibility.

**So you don't feel that comedians' being neurotic
makes your job more difficult?**

No. They're neurotic. We're neurotic. Any job is
difficult. If I had to stand in Woolworth's or Macy's
all day, that would be hard. I'm sure it's hard for
salesladies, because I know what their reaction is to
me when I come in. If you have to work for a living,
you're in trouble. I don't care what you do. The
comedian, the writer, the fellow who brings the
sandwiches—you're in trouble.

**For the fledgling comedy writer, is there any value
in reading Thurber, Benchley, Perelman, and the
other great humorists?**

I don't care what you're going to be when you
grow up; reading is the greatest thing in the whole
world. I find it stimulating. I reread Benchley and
Thurber. Reading is very important and relation-
ships with people.

**You mentioned before that great comedy is based on
truth. Sid Caesar said, "The truer it is the funnier it
is." Is truthful comedy the same as satire?**

That's very interesting. They talk about one
thing being satirical and one thing being a farce. It's
very hard for me to put labels on anything because I
don't know exactly what that means. When Sid
Caesar and Imogene Coca did a sketch of a PTA

meeting, it was a reflection of our times. It was funny because that's what comedy is. Good comedy writing is a reflection of our times.

In an article on comedy writers *Time* magazine once quoted a research project that said, "Most comedians are not qualified judges of the kind of material they should use." Has this been your experience?

No. The guy wouldn't be a top comedian if he didn't know what was right for him. It isn't always one hundred percent, but then who's right all the time? It's like the example we once talked about: The writer handed in six pages, and only two pages turned out good. He thought he was handing in six funny pages. The comedian thinks that he's absolutely right about what he's picking. But he's got to have that feeling, that confidence, because he's the one who's got to go out on stage and face the audience. That's why they surround themselves with talented writers who sometimes can persuade them to try something. At best, you're guessing. If you're an expert, you're just guessing a little better than somebody who is not an expert. You know as a performer you can do the same jokes at a nine o'clock show and get one reaction, do that same thing at the twelve o'clock show and it's hilarious. There are a thousand reasons a joke will be funny one time and not another.

You've appeared as a guest on many television shows. Is that easier than writing comedy?

Oh, yeah. I appear on panel shows because it's fun. I like the acceptance. My approach is different. I'm not doing that for a living. When you're writing for a living you're sweating. I have fun when I write jokes, except it is involved with wanting to keep your job and having to pay your rent. You've got all that pressure. When I'm sitting around on those panel shows it's as if I'm going to a party.

Do you prepare what you are going to say?

I'd rather not. I have more fun when something happens and we can kick it around. If I prepared it then I would have to be conscious of what I'm saying, and then I'd have to rehearse and remember it.

What is it that prevents so many comedy writers from performing their own material?

Gee, I don't know. They just haven't any guts. Jack Paar used to ask me to go on and I'd say, "What will I do up there? I'm not a performer; I'm not a comedian." And he would say, "We'll just sit around and talk the way we do when we're sitting around the Cromwell Drug Store." So I finally agreed and I went. I didn't think I was going to like it, and now I like it. It's acceptance. You know as a performer how wonderful that is.

Do you find the acceptance as a performer more gratifying than the enjoyment of creating a comedy line?

I'm so happy with acceptance. When I walk in and the butcher recognizes me, I'm happy. We all want to be accepted. What's the use of kidding about it?

How much of a writer's success depends on having a good agent?

You need an agent to get you your first job. An agent is a strange thing. Once people know you in the business they will call you, but you need an agent to negotiate the contract. What they do to performers is frightening. It's a necessary evil in this business.

Jack
DOUGLAS

Jack Douglas was born Douglas Crickard in
Tahiti, the son of an actress who sang in Victor
Herbert operettas. His father was a cable engineer.
Douglas grew up on Long Island and attended Mer-
cersbury Academy in preparation for Princeton
University, but he elected to dispense with the prep-
aration as well as the college education.

He started in show business as a drummer with
Al Vann and his orchestra. Afterward, he worked in
musical films as a chorus boy: *Whoopie,* starring
Eddie Cantor, and *Reaching for the Moon,* with
Douglas Fairbanks, Sr.

The comic-turned-writer (he once was a gorilla
for Olson and Johnson) began his writing career in
1938 with Bob Hope and since then has created
comedy for Bing Crosby, Red Skelton, Jack Carson,
Johnny Carson, George Gobel, and, of course, Jack
Paar.

Douglas is a sports car racing buff. He has
collected over fifty trophies and at one time was the
number five man in the country.

He is married to the Oriental singing star Reiko,

and they have two sons, Timothy and Bobby. The Douglases make their home in Canada and Connecticut.

Douglas has written for most of the major radio and television shows, published magazine articles, and performed in nightclubs as well as on records with his comedy album for Columbia, *Jack Douglas with the Original Cast.*

His books include:

Benedict Arnold Slept Here
The Jewish-Japanese Sex & Cook Book and *How to Raise Wolves*
What Do You Hear from Walden Pond?
Shut Up and Eat Your Snowshoes
The Neighbors Are Scaring My Wolf
The Adventures of Huckleberry Hashimoto
A Funny Thing Happened to Me on My Way to the Grave
Never Trust a Naked Bus Driver
My Brother Was an Only Child

The distance from my typewriter in Hollywood to Jack Douglas's Connecticut mountaintop retreat is exactly 2,932 miles. The last mile and a half winds up a narrow dirt and rock-paved road bounded on both sides by summer-thick foliage.

Once at the Douglases' three-level frame house, you relax in the spacious living room and look across several vibrantly verdant hills into New York State. The second floor is devoted to bedrooms. On the third is an office bulging with shelves of books, scripts, and papers.

Douglas's desk is a twelve-by-five piece of plywood set on two wooden horses. On its center rests a 1930 Remington typewriter (Douglas types with two fingers). There is a bulletin board clogged with clippings, notes, and scraps of information. A large Colt .45 in a holster is lying near the typewriter. In the hall stairway, racked on the wall, are a .22 Ruger, a Colt AR15, and a Japanese twenty-pound rifle.

In back of the house is a large fenced area in which are caged Douglas's two loving pets—Pussycat, a three-year-old cougar, and Tonuki, a silver-gray mammoth wolf.

Jack Douglas has a disarming, informal manner and is perhaps the shyest of all the writers interviewed. He wears prescription sunglasses, even in the house, and pauses before answering questions. He is rather serious but smiles easily, revealing two rows of fine, straight teeth.

His skin is clear and his jaw firm. He is tall, well built and in excellent physical condition. Dressed in a simple white sport shirt, tan corduroys, and heavy brown leather climbing boots, Douglas looks the true outdoorsman.

He gives the impression of having spent his life working diligently at his trade but never having taken time out to analyze how or why.

Reiko, the thoughtful and gracious hostess, was kind enough to prepare lunch after my long plane and car journey. It was a typical Oriental meal prepared by a beautiful Japanese housewife—a ham and cheese sandwich and coke!

In A Funny Thing Happened to Me on My Way to the Grave, **you said you first started writing comedy in 1939. What had you done in comedy prior to that?**

I had done nightclub stuff. That is, I had been a performer. First I was a drummer, then a band comic. Then I did straight monologues. A stand-up comic in clubs, theaters. Went to England . . .
Did you write your own material?

Yeah, that's right. There's no doubt I swiped a few things, too. My first vaudeville date was at the Academy of Music on Fourteenth Street in New York. I was a drummer. We worked with a lot of comedians, like Richie Craig. We backed those guys up. And in those days a drummer had to sing. This was before 1930.

Did you read music?

I read. Not the greatest. I studied music, but I really can't say I was great at it.

After watching comedians for a while as the drummer—

I went to California. I played places in Culver City, played for dancing, and I also did table singing. Then I started doing funny stuff. I got a job in the Cotton Club. Lionel Hampton was the drummer there. I sang, did crazy things—poetry, weird stuff. Buddy Rogers came into the place one night; he was forming a band. So I went with him, and I started doing stand-up. Then after a while I did away with that and just became the comic with the band.

What was it that made you decide to stop being a comedian and start writing for other comedians?

I met Bob Hope and started doing his act.

You stole his act?

No, I didn't steal it. Hope went to Broadway to do a show, so he sent me out with his brother George, and we did Bob's act, word for word. George would sit out in the theater in a box. George's wife was the stooge on the stage.

Like a heckler routine.

Yeah. Well, I was friendly with Hope from those days. Then when he came to Hollywood he started "The Pepsodent Show"—I think it was 1938 or '39. I bumped into him on the street and he said, "I'm starting a show for Pepsodent. How'd you like to write a few things for me?" He offered me fifty bucks a week and I said, "No. Sixty!" I was bold as brass. I didn't have a freaking quarter. We haggled back and forth. I finally got sixty dollars out of him. That's how it started. Of course, we got raises as time went on, and I stayed.

You said in the book that Hope's show was the greatest training a comedy writer could get. Why was that?

Because we had competition writing. At the beginning *everybody* wrote the whole show. We all wrote monologues. Then we had the guest spots. Judy Garland was on a lot of them. Then at the end we'd have a song sketch. We'd start a song like "Yes Sir, That's My Baby," go out of that into a sketch about maternity hospitals.

But the competition was pretty strong. We had guys like Jack Rose, Mel Shavelson, Milt Josefsberg, Norman Panama, and Melvin Frank and Norman Sullivan—who's still with Hope. Hope decided that teams would write forty pages and single guys would write twenty pages. That's twenty pages of everything, including the monologue.

Well, Hope had over a hundred and sixty pages of stuff to choose from. He'd listen to each guy's monologue and check off the jokes he liked. If you had five jokes in the final monologue you were the hero of the week. Sometimes you'd get lucky and have a lot more, because he used a lot of jokes.

At this point, had you developed any style or formula for writing? Were there certain techniques you knew would work?

I had a style which was mostly the wild and bizarre. Hope used to call me "the Mad Dog." That was one of his pet names for me. He had very affectionate qualities, until we had a fight one time. After that he didn't speak to me for almost ten years. But whatever my style was, it was something he liked.

Did you begin to notice that Hope had a rhythm in his one-line jokes? Did you begin to pattern your material to match his delivery?

Well, not the pattern as much as the subject. As an example, if he got flipped on jokes about the vice-president or women's lib . . .

He wanted something on a specific subject?

Yeah. We would just read the papers or magazines to get the subject matter.

Were there certain formulas or techniques that you developed as a result of writing for Hope?

Well, the only formula I had was that I always wrote myself into a corner. In other words, I'd use a straight line and try to figure out an answer for it. For example, why are you wearing a brown shirt? I'd try to find a funny answer.

It was white originally, but my wife washed it with my socks.

Yeah, whatever the joke is.

This was something you trained yourself to do?

Yeah.

Suppose Hope wanted to do jokes on Rudy Vallee and you wrote the straight line: "Rudy Vallee has the biggest megaphone in California . . ."

It's really not a megaphone—it's his lips.

So your technique was to write a straight line and then try to come up with a second sentence that was funny.

Yeah. And also there was a series of three. A joke, a topper, and a second topper.

What does that mean?

You write the joke. Then you do another joke to top the first one. Then you write still another funny line to top the second one.

Why is that?

I don't know. But that seems to be a formula that works for a lot of comedians. It's a magic thing. **Perhaps the reason is that when you get a laugh and you top it and then you top it again you have a roll going. And it makes the other jokes after that easier for the audience to digest because you've got them laughing.**

And not only that. The two toppers sound like ad-libs. It's the greatest thing for an audience to think you haven't got a routine, that you're doing it all off the top of your head.

We just talked about the "one liner." What about the construction of a joke that has three or four sentences?

When I say one-liner, I am talking about a monologue. In a sketch, that's something different. In radio you not only had words; you had sound effects. On "The Bob Hope Show" we had certain people we relied on—Brenda and Cobina, Jerry Colonna . . .

You built sketches around the characters that were signed to do the show with Hope?

That's right. We'd go to Jerry Colonna for a few jokes. He'd call from Detroit. He had that Yehudi line, which was mine. "Who's Yehudi?" Yehudi Menuhin was first becoming prominent. Then a few jokes with Brenda and Cobina.

You said you wrote a sentence and then tried to get a funny answer. Could you describe the mental process you went through to get what you thought would be funny?

Oh, boy! I don't think so. How many books have been written about that? Max Eastman did one, *The Enjoyment of Laughter*. That was about what makes people laugh.

Let's create a sentence: "From this view, we can see Connecticut, Massachusetts, and New York . . ."

You can also see the guy coming up from the bank to collect for the mortgage. There's the joke: "We got a beautiful house on the hill. We can see New York, Connecticut, Massachusetts, and the man from the finance company. Add the word *expensive* to the straight line. That helps it. "We own an *expensive* house on the hill, et cetera."

So the process for you is to make a serious or straight statement first. Then follow it with a ludicrous or ridiculous comment, which hopefully comes out a joke.

Yeah. I think so. When you're trying for a laugh it's hard to explain. I think you either have the talent to do it or you don't.

Suppose we were sitting here with a carpenter. He might say, "This is an expensive house, but what a view. You can see New York, Connecticut, and Massachusetts." And he would end the statement there. But Jack Douglas adds a funny line by saying . . .

Stop looking out the window and get back up there on that ladder.

That's still another punch line.

Yeah.

So the difference between the person who sees only what is there—the unvarnished, straight situation—and the comedy writer is that the comedic mind turns that situation into a joke!

That's right.

You said, you either have the talent or you don't. Is the ability to write funny lines a craft that anybody can learn, or did you mean you are born with it?

I don't know whether you're born with it or not. My mother's side of the family were all on the stage, and my mother did comedy. My grandfather did comedy. On the legitimate stage, not vaudeville. Did I inherit something from them? I don't feel that I did, really, because they didn't want me to do anything like this. Writing they had never thought of. Being on the stage? Most actors don't want their kids to be on the stage because they know how goddamn rough it is. I think it was a matter of. . . It seems to me that all my life I've been kidded about everything. Not in a nasty way, not in an ethnic way, because I was not in an ethnic group that was being kidded. So I was lucky that way. I've always been kidded. I don't even know why.

A good percentage of comedy writers are Jewish or members of a minority group, and you're not.

That's right.

It seems the motivating factors for entering comedy are coming from an impoverished background, being a member of a minority, or growing up in a family environment where there was not much love.

Yeah.

Have you ever thought about it like that?

I thought about that, but I didn't come from an impoverished background. We were never rich, nowhere near it. And not even from an ethnic group that got put down by anybody. I was not on the defensive or belligerent. I wasn't a fat kid. I wasn't anything. When I was in high school I was a football player and a runner. I was a big high school hero, so I had nothing going that way. Where they could say,

"This guy's got a club foot," or "He's humpbacked," or "He's a Jewish humpbacked Negro." There was none of that with me.

But people have always kidded me. To this day I go to the hardware store and the guy will say something. I bought a chain saw and it starts to leak. I'm just using this as an example—it didn't happen this way. But the owner will say, "Yeah, it figured. You buying a chain saw; something had to go wrong." Why do people say things like that to me? I don't know why.

Sometimes we project ineptness. Maybe we don't exert aggressiveness and people sense that.

Yeah, I can see that.

Arnold Auerbach, in his book _Funnymen Don't Laugh,_ describes his apprenticeship as a comedy writer. The man he worked for sent him to the library, and for months Auerbach did nothing but copy jokes and arrange them in a file till he got the feeling of construction of jokes. Other than writing for Hope, did you ever make any conscious effort to develop your craft?

No. I used to admire Benchley. I read him. I bought a book called _The Encyclopedia of Comedy._ It was full of end men's jokes for minstrel shows. I bought the book with the idea of trying to learn something. I didn't. I never bought a book on how to write comedy or anything like that. It just evolved from being a drummer.

Is it possible that aside from being able to see things funny your ability developed through your experiences? First, you were a drummer and listened to comedians week in and week out. Then you got a job where you were forced to come up with new jokes every week. You rubbed elbows with other writers.

Perhaps you absorbed all this and then by trial and error learned how to create jokes.

I'm sure. Absolutely right. Because I don't think I really was too fond of writing jokes for myself.

As a result of watching so many comedians, you may have absorbed joke construction. It seeped into your unconscious, and then—

There's no doubt about it.

—and then later on you dredged up that information and used it.

Oh, yeah.

Do comedians have a good idea of what's funny and what will work for them?

It depends. If you told Bob Hope something was funny he'd go out and give it a try and give it everything he had, and if it didn't get a laugh, then it was the fault of the joke. But you do that with Skelton, he'd just dog it or leave out a word.

What about Jack Paar?

Well, Paar, when he's rolling, he's very reliable on jokes. Here's the arrangement I had with Paar. I'd just give him the sheets of paper and let him pick what he liked. And he never said, "How about another so-and-so." He'd say, "How about doing something on Bobby Kennedy." That's when he did a monologue. He would ask for a few jokes. But he would never say "boo" about what you did. He would never criticize.

Then your relationship with most comedians you've worked for has been basically a good one?

Oh, yeah. I haven't really worked with that many, but they were always very friendly. I only had one lawsuit with Garry Moore and Jimmy Durante. They figured they were paying me too much money. We finally settled it.

Is it important for a comedy writer to be well read?
I think so. For one reason only: to stimulate your brain. Have you ever gone a couple of weeks without reading a goddamn thing? You get dumb. I don't read Max Shulman because I don't want to copy anything. I started to read *Rally Round the Flag, Boys* and I said to myself, "This guy's awful close to the way I think, and I don't want to get into a sweat." I never did read him. In the old days I used to read S. J. Perelman.

What do you do about getting bogged down when you're writing?
There's one thing I do that I haven't done lately, and I better start in again. I get up at quarter to four in the morning. I get my coffee. I go to my room upstairs, sit down, and I write. Just belt! Just write! I don't think; I don't do a goddamn thing; I just write. And this isn't trying to make myself out a genius; that's just the way it goes. If I sit down and have coffee, take one of the animals for a walk, come back, and then go up to work at nine-thirty or ten in the morning—nothing! I'll be able to work only for an hour or so, and that's it.

You can't do it?
There's nothing.

Getting up at quarter to four in the morning before it's light out, you find your senses are sharp, and you work until—
Oh, yes; that's right. I work four or five hours straight through. Then I usually take a nap, because I don't go to bed at nine o'clock at night, which I should if I want to keep up this routine. But I don't, because I always stay up and watch some rotten TV movie. But if I didn't stay up late, I wouldn't have to take a nap.

You found through the years that routine was the best for you?

No; I read it in Ripley's "Believe It or Not," or someplace like that. It said some French novelist in the last century used to get up early every morning and by nine o'clock he was finished with his day's work. Left him free all day to go to the cafe, sit around drinking coffee and having a ball. But he'd always be home early. That was their idea of life anyway.

Herman Wouk was one of Fred Allen's writers. Is comedy writing, learning the craft and construction of jokes, a good prerequisite for someone who wants to write fiction?

I think so, yeah. You do have to be observant. You watch people. I try to. Even though I don't do it consciously, I must be doing something, because I remember incidents and how they developed. Doing comedy is a great training ground for straight writing, for straight acting. I don't think it's the other way around. I don't think if you're a straight actor, you can suddenly become a comic.

In *A Funny Thing Happened to Me on the Way to the Grave,* **you wrote that "most comedians have no confidence in the material, themselves, or the audience." How is it possible to write for people who are so unsure and insecure?**

Well, maybe I went too far with that. Bob Hope, for an example. This is not a matter of confidence, because he's got all the confidence in the world when you see him perform, and offstage he's certainly a confident guy—with money to back it up. We did a show with him once—the Carson Show—it was almost like the first time he'd done a show. When he came off, he came up to me with, "How was it? OK?"

Now this to me was damn funny! I've seen Jack Benny do that same thing.

No matter how big a star is he's still worried about being a hit.

That's right.

There's a quote from the same book, "Writing comedy is an art, like plumbing. Once you know how to stop the toilet from overflowing you can do it most every time." Does that mean writing funny comes easy to you?

Writing funny comes easy to me if I get up at quarter to four in the morning and go up there and do it. If I went up there right now or, as I said, at ten o'clock in the morning, it does not come easy. No! Because I have more goddamn things to look at and fool with—maps and books and brochures and crap. Things that distract me.

Then through the discipline of getting your mind and body set every morning at the same time—it works for you.

It has so far. I didn't always do it that way. I remember many times in the radio days you had to hand in a script by noon. That was the deadline. I would get up maybe earlier than four o'clock to write a whole script or a sketch or whatever I was writing. I would put it off until the last minute, then I got up early to do it—so that's probably where that came from, too. That early morning routine.

You've written acts for celebrities. How much time did the act consist of?

Six to ten minutes. It was usually a monologue and little bits.

How many pages would those six to ten minutes be?

On a monologue it would be three to four pages.

Approximately how many individual jokes would be on those four pages?

I cheat on margins to make it look like more, because I write by the pound. I don't write by the joke anymore. If I were writing a book I'd use the whole goddamn page, because I don't want to change the page in the typewriter so often. I'd say about six-seven jokes per page.

Then you give the celebrity approximately thirty jokes. When the star does that material in Las Vegas, what percentage of those thirty jokes work?

I have no way of telling, because I've never seen any of those people work.

When a comedian buys material from a comedy writer, the best he could possibly hope will work is about half.

I'd say about fifty percent is a good average. We'd have to guarantee at least fifty percent.

Now the celebrity, by virtue of being well known to the audience, has a better chance of reaction . . .

He's presold.

. . .than a comedian the audience has never met before.

Oh, yeah. The unknown comedian has to have stronger material.

Say a celebrity who's never done an act—Rock Hudson, for example—wants to do an act in Vegas with six or seven girls, singing and dancing, and he needs thirty jokes for an opening monologue. How would you go about creating the material for him?

I once saw him in a movie, *Pretty Maids All in a Row,* where he screwed everybody in sight. It would be pretty easy to latch onto a thing like that—of course, provided everybody had seen the movie.

Well, I could start him off by having him say, "My name is Rock Hudson. That's the name the studio gave me. I wanted to call myself Troy." In other words, fool around with his name first.

You'd get a biography on him and make a list of all the things you thought would be—

That the people in the audience would know about. I'd jot down some notes, whatever I got out of the biography. I'd put in that he's done so many pictures with Doris Day. Then he could talk about Doris. There are a lot of Doris Day jokes.

Then you'd write jokes based on subjects the public would know about as a result of seeing his movies or reading about him in the newspapers and magazines?

I think that's all you could come up with.

Then in writing material for a celebrity you have to stay within the framework of what he does and what he is?

Not necessarily. For instance, you could start off by saying, "Before I was an actor I was a so-and-so." He could be anything. "I was an Arctic explorer. They wear those big fur coats." And do a joke on that. "Then after that, I was an Avon lady in the gay district." That type of thing.

It's common knowledge that novelists like Fitzgerald and Hemingway were rather substantial drinkers. Is this also a malady among comedy writers?

I think it exists hardly at all among comedy writers. I don't know why. I know only one writer who used to drink quite a bit. Fell off a train in Truckee, California, and got himself run over by a freight train. Used to work for Hope. Fred Williams. He was a very clever guy, but he used to drink. For Chrissake, it finally got to the point where one beer would set him off. He'd be poisoned—an alcoholic.

The novelists claimed they drank to relax, to be able to create more easily. Certainly there is the same amount of energy required to write jokes, and yet

the majority of comedy writers do not drink. Why do you think that is?

I don't know. They're all pretty sober. Tennessee Williams drinks like a fish. Faulkner used to lie down with a teeny pad, they tell me. He'd write on those teeny papers and throw them on the floor as he finished, and he'd be sitting there with a bottle. That's something I heard.

But, Jesus, that's a good question. I used to drink pretty good myself. But it was always like—after you finished the show, you go out and get loaded. That was the reward almost. I quit drinking a hell of a long time ago.

About your book Shut Up and Eat Your Snowshoes—**How many drafts did you have to write before it went to the publishers?**

Well, I didn't write any drafts. Just one. Then I changed it. I don't write drafts. They cut out the parts they didn't like.

Did you write an outline for the book before you started?

No. I've tried outlines three or four times, and I never sold a book from an outline. I can't do them. I have some outlines upstairs for movies—in Hollywood they call them treatments. You wouldn't make a movie out of some of those things that became big pictures. I wouldn't do it. I wouldn't put fifteen cents in some of them. They're just bullshit outlines is what they are. But I suppose somebody has to have something to show somebody. I know I could write a good book on a couple of the outlines I wrote, but I have no interest.

How long did it take to write Snowshoes?

I figure six months. That isn't every day, that's—

From quarter to four in the morning until a little after nine.

Yeah, and then it's handing it in and then after they fool around with it for a couple of weeks and then you get it back. Oh, it could be done in three months if you really—

Three months? Five days a week? Four hours a day?

Well, I work every day. When I work, I work seven days a week. Even when I'm on so-called vacations, I don't stop. I just can't lay off.

You get a contented feeling of accomplishment about finishing four hours' work.

Oh, sure.

Then whether you're going fishing or taking your wife to the supermarket, you know you've got it done.

That's right.

Even if you've improved the manuscript by adding a couple of words, or you only do a few pages, there's great satisfaction.

Oh, yeah. It's terrible when I don't do . . . like today I haven't done a hell of a lot. Not because of you particularly. But it's Sunday. But that doesn't make any difference to me; I don't care what day it is. I wanted the day to feel easy.

Are there any words of counsel you could give to someone starting out as a comedy writer?

It's tough for the new guy. What do you do with the material after you write it? Who do you give it to? Dick Cavett used to hang around NBC. Jack Paar backs this story up. Cavett just buttonholed him one day and gave him some material and said, "Please read it!" Doing a thing like that to Paar! Holy Christ! He'd fall apart completely. But somehow he read it, and he liked it, and that's how Cavett got the job with Paar, and that's how he got started.

So aside from the initiative to write jokes, you must also have the ability, the aggressiveness to go out and sell them?

That's the whole thing. I get stuff in the mail—scripts and things—some of it written in longhand. It's pitiful. You don't know what to say to them. There'd be one joke on the page. It's like a would-be song writer who writes one song. This is his *master-piece*. And he's so shocked that nobody will buy it. It might be a great song—who the hell ever knows—but it's just *one* song.

You mean if he were a professional he'd have a bunch of songs and keep writing until he did sell them.

That's right. Years ago, I remember watching Mack Gordon and a guy he used to work with. I've forgotten his name now. They wrote *Did You Ever See a Dream Walking?* and big songs that are still played today. Well, they were at Catalina Island this particular day, and they sat at the piano and said, "Give us a subject!" Somebody'd yell: "Seashell!" And they'd write a song about a seashell. About a sea gull. About a girl, a boy. Boom, boom, boom. One song right after the other, because they were professionals.

Then to be successful it's a question of how much drive the writer has to keep writing day in and day out despite failures, despite rejections?

That's right. Sinclair Lewis, the first thing he sold, the story goes, was a cake recipe. After he had written some pretty good books. Nobody bought the goddamn things. Well, you can imagine, sitting up here and mailing stuff to the *New Yorker* and other magazines and having those things come back day after day. I tried that years and years ago. I sold something to *Whizbang* or one of those magazines. A one-paragraph story. I got rejections from an awful lot of them.

What's easier to write—one of the humorous books, jokes for a stand-up comedian, or jokes for a TV show like "Laugh-In"?

The "Laugh-In" thing was easy. Of course, I did it from here. That's one of the drawbacks of doing it every year. I know what happens out on the Coast. They say, "Jesus Christ, he sits back there on his ass. He's not at meetings." And so forth. But that's the easiest thing to do.

Is writing a book the most difficult?

Not really, no. No.

There's a difference in the comedy that's written to be read and that which is written to be spoken.

There's a difference, yeah. It's a rhythmic thing. Everybody's said this. You can write a lot of dialogue forever. In a book, you've got to put it in some kind of frame. You have to describe the people somehow. Those are the difficult things in writing a book. But the dialogue can be exactly the same as what you'd write for a monologue or a sketch.

I get letters all the time from people who want to write. How do you go about it and so forth? If you have to ask questions on how you go about it, I don't think you're ever going to make it.

If they were capable of doing it they would?

I think so.

Hal
KANTER

Hal Kanter was born in Savannah, Georgia, on December 18, 1918. He was educated at the Jewish Educational Alliance in Savannah, the Santa Clara Elementary School, the Robert E. Lee Junior High School in Miami, Florida, the Long Beach, New York, High School, the Art Students League of New York, and the Federal Art Project, NYC, and he took extra courses at the University of Kansas at Lawrence, Kansas.

While in the army he took Army Educational Service courses in literature, English, poetry, and theater arts.

Kanter began his career as a cartoonist and then broke into radio as a gag writer for comedy-variety shows. He wrote for Danny Kaye, Jack Paar, and Ed Wynn, and then, in 1951, he was hired by RKO as a screenwriter for *Two Tickets to Broadway* (Tony Martin and Janet Leigh were the stars). Kanter since has written over twenty motion pictures, of which the following classics are just a few:

My Favorite Spy (Paramount; Bob Hope, Hedy Lamarr)

The Road to Bali (Paramount; Bob Hope, Bing Crosby)

The Rose Tattoo (Paramount; Burt Lancaster, Anna Magnani)

Artists and Models (Paramount; Dean Martin, Jerry Lewis)

Dear Brigitte (Twentieth Century; James Stewart)

Here Come the Girls (Paramount; Bob Hope)

Casanova's Big Night (Paramount; Bob Hope, Joan Fontaine)

Bachelor in Paradise (MGM: Bob Hope, Lana Turner)

Money from Home (Paramount; Dean Martin, Jerry Lewis)

Move Over Darling (Twentieth Century; Doris Day, James Garner)

For television, he created, produced, and staged "The George Gobel Show," for which he won an Emmy as writer. From then on Kanter rang up a phenomenal list of credits in television, including the award-winning "Julia," starring Diahann Carroll. Kanter, long associated with the Academy Awards show, also worked on the recent telecast. It was his sixteenth assignment.

Another astounding accomplishment in the career of this fertile framer of verbal funnies is that Hal Kanter has also served as producer and director as well as the creator and writer of many of the shows he has been connected with.

He is presently the executive producer of "All in the Family."

Kanter married the former Doris Prouder (one time merchandising editor of *Parent's Magazine*) in

1941. They have three daughters: Lisa, Donna, and Abigail.

Hal Kanter lives in a sprawling ranch-style house in the San Fernando Valley, California. It is surrounded with lush orange, lemon, and lime trees. The citrus fruit colors pervade the huge, tastefully decorated living room where this interview took place.

Kanter is a six-foot-one, two-hundred-pounder, with distinguished gray hair and sideburns that sharply contrast with a thick dark mustache. He wore a blue denim suit, a white turtleneck sweater, and black boots.

Hal Kanter is witty and literate and speaks with professorial assurance. His answers come easily, almost as if comedy is the very marrow of his enormous talent.

You started writing for the Jack Oakie Show.

That's right. I had encountered Hugh Wedlock and his partner, the late Howard Snyder, and they gave me an opportunity to work with them. They were the co-writers.

Then that was your first professional job in comedy.

Yes, except that prior to that I had been a cartoonist and had sold a lot of cartoons. That's what gave me the idea that I was able to think in terms of comedy. In those days the editors of magazines and newspapers would often buy the idea from a rough drawing or just take the joke in some instances, and then assign it to one of their more established cartoonists. It was, in a sense, a form of ghost writing. In fact, I'd ghost-written a comic strip, too, when I was seventeen.

A cartoon usually causes one to smile or chuckle, whereas a gag is created to evoke a laugh. Still you felt you could write jokes as a result of your cartoon experience?

You'll find that a great many comedy writers who became successful in radio and/or films or television actually began as cartoonists. Bill Morrow, one of the best comedy writers we ever had in this business, had been a cartoonist at one time. David Swift drew for Disney. Don Quinn, the man who created Fibber McGee and Molly, and probably the original folklore humorist of broadcasting, was a cartoonist and continued to draw until his death. There were many others.

Years ago, either on the old *New York Telegram* or the *World,* there was a pixie named Will B. Johnstone who did a daily comic strip based on the news. He was the man who created the popular cartoon figure of the taxpayer wearing a barrel. And summertimes, when he was on vacation from the paper, he used to come here to Hollywood and write Marx Brothers movies. If you look at some of the old ones you will see his screen credit. Groucho, who admires writers, remembers him well.

Then that experience in coming up with a funny idea and putting it down on paper with a picture and a caption gave you the background, some know-how in creating a joke?

I would assume that's true, because cartooning stimulates you into thinking in the briefest possible terms. A cartoon, to be effective, is uncluttered—a simple drawing of a situation with the caption the briefest of statements. That, to me, is quite often the essence of humor. If you can express what's funny succinctly and still get in all the facts, it makes for better humor than a rambling storytelling technique which often can obscure the point you're attempting to make. Amateurs do that often, especially at cocktail parties. And I'm doing it now.

When you began working with Snyder and Wedlock on the Jack Oakie show, what did you discover about this new medium that you weren't aware of as a creator of cartoons?

Well, it was fun. I enjoyed it a great deal. I discovered that writing comedy was easier than doing cartoons because you don't have to draw. Drawing takes a lot of time. Also, the camaraderie that existed among comedy writers of that time I found refreshing and joyous. It was easier than sitting alone in a room wondering what's funny. At least when I was with those fellows I found out instantly what was funny and what wasn't. There's no time for diplomacy when you face a deadline.

Did you discover the technique of writing a joke?

Technique? What I discovered was a lot of basic formulas that existed at the time. A great deal of radio comedy—in those days particularly—was very formularized. There were certain basic jokes and approaches to jokes that people kept doing over and over and over again.

For example?

I wish I could crystallize it and cite an example. I'd have to do some thinking, because I have trained myself over the years to rid my mind of all those old clichés and old notions. And you seldom encounter them anymore.

Is that because comedy has changed so much that those formulas are no longer of any value?

I think they're of value in some instances, but I don't think they're used quite as much, quite as obviously, today. Comedy has changed considerably; it's much more character comedy now. In the old days when you wrote radio jokes that generated laughter from an audience, very often you could take that same script and just by altering a word here or there, or changing names, almost anybody in radio could do it. A Joe Penner joke worked for Judy Canova, for example. One of the complaints about radio comedy in those days was a kind of sameness that existed. You would hear the same joke on six different shows, with very slight variations, if any at all.

I remember the first time that happened to me. They were talking about Anna Held and the milk bath. And I had a line about "a country girl who took a milk shower every day. She had a very tall cow." That joke got a very big laugh at that time. Now, I was shocked when I heard this same joke repeated on three different shows within two weeks after it had been exposed. New guys came along, men like Sherwood Schwartz, Phil Leslie, Phil Sharp and Nate Monaster and Sol Saks—they changed that little by little.

Now, in New York there were several people— and I was very friendly with one of them—who made it a point to sit beside a radio every night of the week and write in longhand on a yellow pad every joke that got a laugh. The man I knew would then take those jokes over to Loew's State or the Palace Theatre and sell them to the comics who were working. He made a living doing that. As a writer, he was about as inventive as a scream from a dentist's office. He was the original Xerox machine.

Would a joke that you or one of the comedy writers

created for a radio show still work as well for the comedian on stage?

Usually, if it was funny. The one thing that the comedian on stage has going for him is the ability to edit material. If he is offered ten jokes, he will know which ones he felt he could use effectively. In those days the truly original shows had character comedy going for them. They were unique. Jack Benny is a perfect example of it. Even though he did great jokes, there were many that somebody else could not do because they were so peculiar to his character. Today, there are very few jokes you can steal from television situation comedy and sell to anybody else, because most are so indigenous to the character and that set of circumstances, they would be meaningless in somebody else's mouth.

After the service you wrote for Danny Kaye under Goodman Ace, and those were still your formative years in comedy writing. Would you agree?

I would suppose so, yeah. Of course, what you have skipped over biographically is that I spent close to five years in the army, and during that period I did a tremendous amount of writing— constantly. Here, and overseas especially. That was all I was doing, practically, once basic training was over. The Armed Forces Radio, particularly, was just a constant battle to fill air time with material. Not only comedy, but documentaries and news, everything. I wrote literally more than I could lift, to quote Fred Allen.

After the service, when you started writing again in show business, what kind of joke techniques were you beginning to develop?

Well, one thing from working with Goody, I

began to learn the value of literacy more and more. Goody is a very well read, very intelligent, and articulate man, and he insisted on a certain level of literacy in the scripts we prepared for Danny. Danny, fortunately, was able to accommodate that point of view.

And because we were exposed to a great many different guest artists, I learned to accommodate myself to them. Luckily, I always had a pretty good ear so that I could get the sense of the swing, the way a Jimmy Stewart delivers a line as opposed to a Jimmy Durante, for instance. I think that's of great value to anybody attempting to write for established personalities. It is much easier to do that than to take a complete unknown and develop a style for him, or to develop a new personality.

The importance of having a good ear—what exactly does that entail?

It's attention to tonal detail. It's almost intuitive, I guess. Either one has it or one doesn't. I suppose one could develop an ear by listening and by observing. Quite often my interpretation of an artist is what the general public assumes him to be rather than what he really is. Therefore, by being an intelligent listener one could become a more intelligent writer.

How about the word *aware*, a more aware listener?

That's better. You are aware that I'm not really that intelligent.

Then in those days, let's say, if Jimmy Stewart were a guest on the show, by virtue of listening to his speech pattern, his rhythm, you were able to write his dialogue more easily?

Exactly. One example comes immediately to mind. We were working on a script for a show where the guest was Fred Allen. Fred had always been an idol of mine. I loved Fred's humor, his sarcasm, his wit, his sense of satire, his impishness and his language—apart from the fact that I considered him to be one of the most original, inventive comedy minds I had ever encountered. I didn't even know the man at the time. Now I'm going to write something for him for the first time. I began to phrase the dialogue in the cadences and vocabulary that I assumed Fred would use, and the guy in charge said, "Fred doesn't talk like that. It's too cluttered. There are too many big words. Take this out, take that out. Let's get down to the essence; let's get to the joke."

So he rewrote a section that I had written. When Fred came in and picked up the script for the first time, he liked it very much, but he said, "May I make a few changes?" And, of course, no one's going to say "No" to the mighty Allen. Fred then began to put into the script much of the sort of language I had originally written and which had been taken out. This vindicated my point of view, I felt. As a result, Fred and I became very dear friends. That's an example of what I mean by having an ear. Now obviously the man who was my head writer at the time, or my producer, whatever he was, did not have the same ear, the same awareness that I had fortunately developed. Thanks for the use of your word. Aware.

He was primarily concerned with the joke, making sure that the script was funny. Then if his boss wanted to put in more words he felt he still did his job. You were going beyond that point.

I think so. I must also say that he was absolutely correct about many other things I was wrong about.

In an interview with John Crosby for the article "No Laughing Matter," you were quoted as saying, "The

**basic common denominators for jokes are the little
things everyone knows about." What exactly did you
mean?**

Well, I think at that time we probably were
talking about the George Gobel Show. I was trying
to find out why George was doing so well. I think it's
because, rather than deal with the usual jokes that
most comedy writers were writing in those days,
jokes about golf or mothers-in-law, or ones with
oblique references to sex and so forth, we talked
about the minutiae of life, things like getting a green
shade for a bathroom. I think Harry Winkler did a
joke on that. Just that little point of recognition.
People suddenly remembered, "Oh yes; the old days
when they'd have a green shade in the bathroom in
the apartment house back East." We talked about
emptying the water from under the ice box, the drip
pan people had long since forgotten about. But little
tiny things, like pocket lint, toothbrushes. Jack
Douglas does a lot of that, outrageously.

Things that people could identify with.

Exactly. They said, "My God, that's right. You
know, that's true." Everett Greenbaum is a master
miner of that vein of golden fun, less manic than
Doug.

**What does a new writer have to do today—someone
just coming up—to be aware of the "little things
everyone knows about"?**

I think every writer coming along is aware of
those little things that everybody knows about. I
think that the new young writers I've met in the past
few years seem to be much more sophisticated and
much better educated and much more aware than
many of the early-day joke writers. The latter kind
of fell into it because they were funny kids on the

street and never quite made it as stand-up comics. They did the next best thing, which was to sell their jokes or whatever to other comedians. But today most people have better educations. Either the school system is responsible or just the constant exposure to the media. Nobody is unaware anymore now that television is everywhere. Just don't get so sophisticated you discard the little honesties of life.

You seem to have more formal education than most of the writers of your era. In what way has this been an advantage to you?

I don't know. I can't answer that. I like to think this is my era still. It makes me a more comfortable person in a lot of circumstances. Sometimes it's a drawback, because I may want to talk about or develop a theme about something that is alien to a large segment of the population, or at least to the people with whom I am dealing, and they may reject it. I don't know that it's really a formal education. It's an informal education that's been acquired primarily by living, looking, listening—by reading, and also by the fact that I have a wife who is very much aware of what is going on in the world. She reads a great deal and brings many things to my attention that I might otherwise overlook completely if I were a bachelor or married to somebody who is less perceptive than she.

There seems to be a difference of opinion among comedy pundits as to the number of different kinds of jokes. What is your opinion?

I've read a great many of these pundits and philosophers, and I don't think any central observation emerges that you can say is true or is a rule. Somebody said there are seven basic jokes; somebody said there are eight basic plots; somebody said there are only twelve jokes. I don't know. I know that I'm constantly amused by something that strikes me as being funny that I've never heard before. Sid Dorfman breaks me up constantly. But I suppose that if you really sat down and analyzed it, you could say, "Oh yes, that is a variation of . . .," and you go back to the original antique. Fred Allen was one who said there were only seven basic jokes, yet I've never been able to trace them and find out what they are. I suppose somewhere somebody's already done that. Some scholarly type like Nat Monaster.

Humor changes so. What's funny to somebody at one point is no longer funny at another point. I remember when jokes about death were always very funny to me. I wrote a lot of them. There was a character on Irving Brecher's old "Life of Riley" show who was a mortician, always doing death jokes. Well, as more of my contemporaries pass and the older I get, the less funny death seems. I saw an episode last night on television where a guy in "Hot L Baltimore" dies in a hooker's apartment. I didn't think it was very funny, really. In fact, I was rather appalled by the whole thing. But there was a time when I'm sure I would have found that hysterical. Maybe someday I will again, if science licks death. Television has evidently already licked hookers. That part I don't mind. Sammy Cahn told me something wise the other night—that every audience is fearful of dying. As entertainers, we're welcome because we make them laugh and for a brief moment they forget they're going to die. Nice, huh? Bullshit, but nice.

What are the other ways in which comedy has changed from those early radio days?

We are much more permissive now in the areas that the writers are allowed to explore for comedy

and drama. The latitudes have expanded: horizons
are farther away, so practically any subject is now
grist for the mill of the comedy writer. That's one
thing. The other is that greater tendency toward
reality in comedy, toward real people, to give characters more substance, more dimension than the old
days. They were mostly cartoon figures then. The
survivors were those who were more than that.
People like Jack Benny who had developed a character continued to survive, continued to be funny to the
last. So did those writers capable of recognizing and
recreating character—Shavelson and Rose, Panama and Frank, Larry Marks and Larry Gelbart, Ed
Hartman, those men.

**As a result of this permissiveness, is it easier for a
comedy writer to create lines today than years ago?**

I think it's easier, yeah! Because you have so
much more to choose from. Now, let's talk about
films for a moment, because films today are pretty
wide open. You can do anything, see anything, show
anything, say anything. As a result, I don't think
that comedy films today are nearly as funny as the
comedy films of twenty, thirty years ago. The reason for that is this: Because there were restrictions,
particularly in terms of sex on the screen, the writer
had to be much, much more inventive in order to
suggest what is going on. Today they just show it
and then make a funny comment. So I think we
have lost something through permissiveness in the
film.

But in television and radio I think we have
gained something, because there are still certain
restrictions that do exist. Even though one is able to
talk about sex, or homosexuality, bestiality, rape,
abortion, almost any of the old taboos you can now
disregard, you still have to be more restricted in

these more public media than you do in motion picture. Therefore, there is still some challenge to creativity.

You feel restrictiveness makes for greater creativity? It forces the comedy writer to create something that is not overt?

Right.

In discussing different kinds of jokes, exaggeration is a common form. Could you give me an example of the way exaggeration works in the development of a joke?

There are so many forms of exaggeration. Seaman Jacobs is great at that form of humor, outrageous exaggeration. Let's see—one instance I was party to—on an old Crosby Show we had Jimmy Durante talking about congressional committees doing all the investigating in Washington. (This is many years ago.) He says, "It's gotten so that everybody is spying on everybody else. Every time you look in a keyhole you get a busy signal." Another example of exaggeration—Jimmy talked about someone who was going to have a birthday party. He said, "The cake was so big they were going to bake it in the Grand Canyon! For candles they're gonna set redwood trees on fire!"

Those are improvements on the basic one-liners: She was so fat that . . . She was so thin that . . .

Yes. That sort of thing seems to be phasing out. You don't hear too many of that kind of joke anymore. The successful comedy today does not deal in that sort of thing. We might take something and exaggerate it all out of proportion in order to dramatize a point, but we'll do a half an hour situation about that. About the need for somebody to lose weight. Instead of saying, "She's so fat that . . . that

she wears the Goodyear blimp for pantyhose," or
whatever the joke is, they now dramatize the whole
thing. Rhoda diets, then discovers her birth control
pills are fattening.

**What's the most difficult part of being a comedy
writer?**

Getting work. One of the most difficult things is
to achieve a unanimity of opinion about what really
is funny before you expose it to the ultimate jury, the
audience. And, quite often, particularly when you
are working in committee, you have many points of
view about what is really funny and what's going to
work and what isn't going to work. I think that's one
of the tough things about it. Both in film and in
television. I haven't been in this so-called free-lance
market where people go from one show to another,
but you hear some real horror stories about the
amount of rewriting being done for one reason or
another.

There are a number of successful shows on the
air now which are completely written by committee.
No matter whose name is on the final screenplay,
it's been gone over by many people. There are probably several reasons for this—insecurity, ego,
genuine difference of opinion as to what is really
funny, or the very strong attitude of an executive
producer who keeps saying, "No, I want it this way."
And if the show is successful you can't very well
argue with that. But, then, there are just as many
comedy shows that are failures because of this
attitude. More! You forget all the shows that have
been shot down.

I remember getting into many discussions
about this in film. Why was there the feeling that it
takes so many writers to turn out a comedy film?

The really classic comedies of all time were all
written by one man—Charlie Chaplin. While Chaplin may have had a gag man (as they called them in
those days) on the set to suggest business here and
there, the total concept was his, and the bulk of the
work quite obviously was his.

The answer to that is, "All right, when you are
Charlie Chaplin, we'll let you do it, too." There aren't
many Chaplins around. But again, you jump forward all the time. Preston Sturgess wrote and
directed some of the most brilliant comedies the
screen has seen. I don't know if you remember many
of those things, but every now and then a guy like
that comes along and is given the opportunity and
he can prove himself and he can do away then with
the so-called committee system of assembling. Mel
Brooks is proving it today. So is Woody Allen. Tati,
in France. Abe Burrows did it once when he had his
own radio show.

**Then you completely disagree with the committee
form—the group writers working toward the end
result?**

I do, yes, in terms of a story line comedy. Definitely in film, where you have more time. I think that
in a variety show it is imperative to have a group of
writers sit around and throw things. George Schlat-
ter, on "Laugh-In," employed Paul Keyes and the
Writers Guild of America, West.

**For many of the TV shows you've been connected
with, you were the writer as well as producer and
director. What are the advantages of serving in all
three capacities?**

You have fewer people to argue with. You are
more apt to get your original concept on the screen
than when you have to go through all those other

channels. Sometimes it works, and sometimes it doesn't. The great advantage to the individual is that he really has total control, and therefore he has much greater responsibility. If he is successful, it's a great ego massage, and if he fails, he can always blame it on the actor, or on the prop man, or Nixon—anybody. Abe Burrows once blamed a flop film on a bank.

So you don't mind that Jerry Lewis has helped write, produce, and direct some of his comedies. But there's a case where it didn't work.

It worked for a while; it worked. Why should I mind? Jerry was very successful for a while and, of course, in France he is still regarded as a genius. The French drink a lot, you know. I think that possibly if he had a little more self-restraint Jerry could continue. He is a very inventive man. I worked on a couple of his earlier films as a writer. I do know that with the proper direction and the proper kind of editing he could have been a great, great star. As a matter of fact, he is a great star in many people's minds, but he could have continued to be, because he is basically a very talented and very funny man.

Editing is self-restraint. Those are key words, particularly in comedy, because one can get involved in excesses and lose all the good one has achieved.

A good comedy director, a good director really serves as an intelligent audience to any intelligent actor. Do you understand what I mean?

No, not exactly.

Me neither. Let's see . . . A good director can observe a scene that's being played and can say, "No, you're going too far here," or "You're not going far enough there"—which is what an audience, in essence, will tell the actor. The director can help the self-starting actor, the comedian. With a really gifted comedy player, and I would say that Jerry Lewis is one, working a scene so that the director who is serving as an intelligent audience—just by the director's reaction to what he's doing, the comedian could know when to stop or how far to go or where to pull back or where to exaggerate. I have worked with directors who very seldom say anything. Norman Z. McLeod was one of them. He was a fine talent, a fine comedy director—incidentally, a former cartoonist, too. Norman seldom spoke to the actors, and when he did he did it very quietly. Men like Hope or Danny Kaye, just by Norman's reaction to what they were doing in blocking out and rehearsing scenes, knew where to stop or where to go.

Then when Jerry is directing his own movie it's impossible for him to do that.

I think that may be a large part of it.

Most of the movies you have written have been for Bob Hope.

Not most. I think I have done about seven.

Is that because you understand his approach to comedy better than others?

Not necessarily. It's because I was under contract to Paramount, for one thing, and did a series of fairly successful films for them. Subsequently I did one for him at Metro based on the fact that I had done those at Paramount. But it was just that circumstance; that's all.

You've also written many of the Academy Awards shows in which Bob Hope was the emcee.

Right.

What are some of the things you keep in mind when you write for him?

Well, with Bob, first of all the monologue is a

compilation of, you know, all of his writers—Mort
Lachman and his staff—plus those of us who are on
the Academy staff. In preparing the other dialogue
or introductions for him, one must remember that
Bob is topical at all times. He's very, very much
today, no matter how old he is chronologically. He
deals with current events, and his attitude is
flip. In the Academy shows—particularly on the
Academy—we characterize him as an eager but
jealous, petulant boy. His attitude is always:
"Nobody really deserves the Oscar as much as I—
and poor me, I never get one." He's always envious
of the handsome movie stars who come on; he's
always just slightly wolfish toward the pretty girls;
and the pretty girls are always insulting him gently
and he accepts that. That's the character one keeps
in mind for Hope's Academy Awards shows.

**And you naturally try to get the jokes to fit those
specific characteristics?**

Right. Because Bob, even though he plays the
put-on comedian who can never be a leading man,
actually looks very elegant on that stage. He's probably better dressed than anybody else there. He
handles himself with aplomb, a sophistication that
few of the others have. You can put him on the stage
with a Rex Harrison, who has this imperial dignity,
and Bob can come up to it. Also, Bob has the stature
now of a world entertainment figure so that no star
who comes on that stage is any bigger than he, and
every star there is aware of it. Even though it may be
their night, they are aware of the fact that Hope is an
institution. He's a kind of monument, you know.

**It is an interesting paradox that you can create lines
about his character even though that character is
really fictitious.**

That's right.

How do you account for that?

I suspect that underneath it, all these characteristics really are his. I suspect that way down deep,
with all of his success, financial and emotional and
social and professional, he really is a little bit
jealous of this one or that one and he really is a little
bit in awe of certain things and—

**That's an interesting aspect of comedians. I have
seen comedy stars hear about another comedian
doing well and turn green with envy. Are comedy
writers like that?**

I don't know. It's difficult to say. I myself am
delighted when most people do well. There are two
people I dislike enormously, and I resent it when
they are doing well, and I am sure that's the general
rule. I don't think there's really that much jealousy
among them.

If you are working on a show with a covey of
comedy writers, there is a desire to have as much of
your material as possible accepted for the final
script, but it is the whole show that is either your
pride or your downfall, you know. Now that I'm in
the fortunate position to be able to pick and choose, I
will work with this group, or this person, or I will
not work. Usually the people I work with are those
whose company I enjoy and whose work I appreciate, and so it's hard to say.

Look, we're all human, and I'm sure that there's
no behavioral law carved in stone. You talk about
comics—I know many comedians who are delighted
when other comedians get laughs. People malign
Milton Berle a great deal. We went through a rough
period together, but I have a great deal of affection
for Milton. I know that when Milton is responsible

for a show—some charity things I've done with him, dinners, and things of that nature—he is ecstatic when somebody gets laughs. He bends over backwards to help.

A good example—he and I were talking before one dinner when he was to be the emcee, and I just happened to mention a joke that I had. It was a very rough, crude joke, and I said, "Do you think this would be all right?"

He said, "Yes, but I'm doing a joke using the same name."

Then I said, "Oh, I'll change it."

And he said, "No, you keep yours, I'll change mine—I'll find a way to change it."

Now that was very, very generous on his part. If Milton Berle were really the kind of person some people accuse him of being he could have, because he preceded me, done the joke and knocked me right out of the box. But he didn't. He did make the change, and he was overjoyed that other people on the dais that night got laughs.

I wonder if the bigger the success the less need there is to prove yourself.

That's a very astute observation.

What is possibly the most rewarding accomplishment that you have had as a writer?

Oh, boy! I keep thinking that the next thing I do is going to be the most rewarding. I keep hoping that that is what it is. There have been a number of things. I was very, very rewarded by the publication of a novel I wrote.

Which was?

A book called *Snake in the Glass,* which Delacorte published a couple of years ago. It didn't sell very well, but it got some marvelous reviews and just the mere fact that what I had written was accepted and published and appears on library shelves all over America is a tremendously rewarding experience to me.

I have a number of friends who have written books, and they begin to take their books for granted, and they can't understand my enthusiasm for mine because they are so anxious to be able to break into films or break into television. So it's what you haven't done but think you're capable of doing that's always the most rewarding when you finally accomplish it.

I'm sure having done "Julia," which was really the first black TV series, was satisfying for you. Didn't that help pave the way for some of the black shows that are now being done?

There's absolutely no question about it. I think it opened doors that had been hermetically sealed as a result of a couple of attempts they had made to do black shows. NBC, I believe it was, tried a variety show starring Nat King Cole. It didn't work; it wasn't accepted, as fine an entertainer as Cole was, and it was a pretty good show as I remember. Sammy Davis never really made it big as a continuing star in a variety series, as brillant an entertainer as Sammy is. He's a show-stopper on any variety show. But when he headed up his own, for some reason it didn't quite work. They had the Beulah show on television, and it was hounded off the air. The Amos 'n' Andy show on television. Amos 'n' Andy had a running gun battle with the NAACP for as long as they have been on the air, for as long as the NAACP has been in business, I guess. So Julia came along at the right time, and it proved that audiences would accept black people in their living room. And while it wasn't nearly as so-called realistic as some of the black shows that have followed, maybe, I still think it was rewarding not only for me but for everybody concerned—for the network, and for the audience itself. Yeah, I'm proud of the Julia show. And of Diahann Carroll, an intelligent and talented beauty. It made her a star beyond Broadway.

With all the permissiveness now, where's comedy heading?

I have no idea. But if you could let me know, I'd like to meet you on the corner when it arrives. I can't picture where it will go. I think it probably is going to swing back to some of the earlier —

The thirties comedies, the Victorian approach?

Not necessarily that, but get back to telling some out-and-out jokes again.

You think the Henny Youngman style is going to come back?

Perhaps. I don't think it's ever going to sweep the country, because Henny Youngman has proved that he's never been able to sweep the country. But there will always be room for that kind of comedy. Crazy jokes, non sequiturs that anyone can repeat.

Do you think there is any peculiarity, any particular quirk in an individual's personality that drives him toward becoming a comedy writer?

I don't know. I think that if you talk to twenty comedy writers, you might find that they all have some basic common denominator. I think you will find twenty highly individual people, too. I find that comedy writers are among the most refreshing and the most inventive, the most alert and the most aware people I know, and I would rather be in their company as a group generally than anyone I know.

Men like Larry Marks, Sid Dorfman, Ev Greenbaum, Milt. Comedy writers and musicians, for some strange reason. They all seem much more sensitive, and I think it is their own sensitivity that makes them good comedy writers, because comedy so often is a defense. Defense against your emotions, your own vision of yourself, the world.

Does that defense include hostility or anger?

Quite often it does, yes. Much comedy is hostility, according to Eastman.

I saw Maurice Chevalier perform twenty-five times over the years, and it never ceased to amaze me how he could continually get laughs without being hostile or angry.

Well, I didn't see him perform that often, but I do remember seeing him at the Greek Theatre here. He did a very funny bit about New Yorkers and Parisians.

The different ways they speak.

Right. Now that, by some people, could be termed hostility, because he was really putting down the way they talk. It's kind of a hostile observation.

Yet the way he did it—

That's the man's own magic and the man's own charm and the man's own personality. But that very same kind of routine . . . I've seen Danny Kaye do similar kinds of things, and Danny is hostile about it. Danny is more acid. I would say if Alan King were to do exactly the same thing it would come out as a cannon shot or a machine gun. It would be overtly hostile . . .

And Rickles, the next step.

Perhaps, yeah. Someone has called him "the Merchant of Venom." I am not particularly a fan of

Rickles, or that kind of comedy. First of all, it's terribly easy to do, just by saying outrageous things about people to their face. Children do that. Drunks. Rickles. You talked about exaggeration before. A lot of what he does is just pure aggressive exaggeration.

You say that kind of comedy is easy to write; then what is the most difficult kind?

Subtlety would be the most difficult. Innuendo. That's one of the things about "Sanford and Son." You know, people hail "Sanford and Son" as the real black experience—well, I doubt that. It's amazing how they get screams when Redd Foxx will turn to the tall woman who plays his sister-in-law and say, "You've got a face like a gorilla and a mouth like a giraffe" or whatever. Just the most common, childish, aggressive statements, and audiences scream at them, in that context. I think that if Cary Grant were to say that to Eve Arden, for instance, it would be a complete—first of all he would never say it, you know—it would be a shock, not a laugh, because it isn't funny. But more power to Sanford as long as they're getting away with it. It's tough enough getting laughs. I'll take "M*A*S*H" and Mary Tyler Moore.

The psychologists in analyzing that would say the audience is getting rid of their frustration in laughing at that kind of thing: "a face like a gorilla."

OK, doctor. I tell you, one of the great successes of the early George Gobel show, I feel, is that George would say things to people in authority that the average man wishes he could think of to say in that same circumstance. That was a great part of his charm, and a great part of his success in those days. It was hostility, but it was kind of understated hostility, and he was polite about it. He never came on like a Don Rickles or an Alan King. I don't say there isn't a place for those two, because quite obviously they have created an enormous place for themselves.

Any suggestions for someone getting started in comedy?

First of all, he should look at as much comedy, investigate and listen to as much comedy as possible and find new areas to approach. invent something new, be as fresh as possible and not try and carbon what already is in existence. There is a great need for laughter in the world. There always will be a need for laughter, and we will always be in need of new writers, new comedians, new performers, new directors. If somebody really wants to write comedy, or to provide laughter, to provoke laughter in some way, nothing is going to stop him. He'll do it. It will happen to him. And depending upon his own taste, his own originality, his own personality, he or she can rise to great heights or can just struggle and stumble along. One never knows what that magic something is that will light the torch, that will attract all the moths in the world, but the opportunity is always there, because I don't think there ever is enough comedy or ever is enough laughter. The field is open as the world is open. As long as there are people, there has to be laughter.

Norman
LEAR

Norman Milton Lear was born on July 27, 1922, in New Haven, Connecticut. After graduating from Weaver High School in Hartford in 1940, Lear attended Emerson College in Boston for a year before enlisting in the United States Air Force in 1942. A technical sergeant in the Fifteenth Air Force stationed near Foggia, Italy, he flew fifty-seven missions as a radioman.

After World War II, in 1946, Lear joined a New York publicity firm. Laid off a year later, he moved to Los Angeles and in time obtained jobs as a comedy writer.

His first film (in partnership with Bud Yorkin) was *Come Blow Your Horn* (Paramount, 1963), starring Frank Sinatra. Adapted by Lear from the Neil Simon play, and directed by Yorkin, it was a box office smash.

The partners, Tandem Productions, Inc., then produced and directed *Never Too Late*. Lear wrote the screenplay for *Divorce American Style* and later collaborated with Arnold Schulman and Sidney Michaels on *The Night They Raided Minskeys*.

In 1971 Lear made his debut as a director with *Cold Turkey* (United Artists), a film he also scripted and produced.

Lear obtained the American rights to "Till Death Do Us Part," a popular BBC-TV series about the English working class, and transformed Alf Garnett, the narrow-minded, prejudiced central character who constantly bickered with his liberal son-in-law, into America's most beloved bigot, Archie Bunker.

"All in the Family" premiered on January 12, 1971, and thus began King Lear's reign as the largest, most successful independent producer in television history.

The following is a list of his shows in production in 1975:

"All in the Family" (CBS; premiere: January 12, 1971)

"Sanford and Son" (NBC; premiere: January 14, 1972)

"Maude" (CBS; premiere: September 12, 1972)

"Good Times" (CBS; premiere: February 8, 1974)

"The Jeffersons" (CBS; premiere: January 18, 1975)

"Hot L Baltimore" (ABC; premiere: January 24, 1975)

Norman Lear married Frances Loeb, a former buyer for Lord and Taylor, in 1956. They live in a colonial-style house in Brentwood, California. The Lears have two daughters, Kate and Maggie.

This session was arranged through a mutual friend, Brad Radnitz, one of television's top writers. The interview was held at the conference table in

Norman Lear's office at CBS Television City in Hollywood.

Lear wore a tan tennis hat, a chocolate-colored turtleneck sweater, beige trousers, and burnished brown hiking boots. Lear is of slight build and medium height with blue eyes and a pale, clean-shaven face. He is quiet, soft-spoken, and gentle-mannered.

Our conversation took place late in the day, and Lear appeared drained from his grueling schedule. (An hour-long meeting with Carroll O'Connor preceded my appointment.) Nevertheless, Lear was gracious and, despite several telephone interruptions, expressed his views with modest sincerity.

At the beginning, who were some of the comedians you wrote for?

The first comedian I wrote for was Danny Thomas. I wrote a routine with Ed Simmons. That was just one piece of special material. Danny Thomas needed a six-minute bit to do at a Friar's Frolic, which is an inside show business affair. We got to him and he did it. A week later we were in New York writing a one-hour television show every week.

That was for—

Jack Haley—"The Jack Haley Show."

Who were some of the comedians after that?

Martin and Lewis—Eddie Simmons and I wrote the Colgate Comedy Hours for three years. Then we did two years of Martha Raye, an hour book musical every week. Then Eddie and I broke up, and I did the George Gobel show for two years.

With Hal Kanter?

No. This was after that half-hour show. I did an hour every week with George. I wrote and directed for two years. And then I went into the movies.

Did you just decide one day that you wanted to be a comedy writer and then begin to seek jobs?

No; I decided one day I wanted to be a press agent. And then another day I found out I couldn't be a press agent and then I started to write.

What kind of background or training did you have that you felt qualified you to begin writing comedy?

I don't know that I felt qualified to begin my comedy writing. In high school I wrote a column called "Notes to You from King Lear." I patterned myself, I recall, after Walter Winchell. The entire column was just as funny as the title. The column was supposed to be funny, so that I can see that the trend was there. So I always wrote and have always enjoyed writing.

How did you get together with Ed Simmons?

We met in Los Angeles when I was trying to become a press agent. The reason I wanted to become a press agent was because I was a depression kid. I had only one uncle who could afford to throw a nephew a quarter. My Uncle Jack was a press agent, and he used to throw me a new quarter every time I saw him. I didn't figure at the time that it was only half a dollar a year. All I ever wanted was to be able to throw a nephew a quarter. I remember that so clearly at thirteen or fourteen. So I knew I had to be like my Uncle Jack. He was a theatrical press agent, so I had to be. Well, getting out of the war I became a theatrical press agent in New York, and the job turned out to be nothing but writing gags for columns.

So that was the beginning of your training in writing jokes and gags, so to speak.

Yeah. Sometimes I would write a full column for Dorothy Kilgallen or Walter Winchell.

**Then you came to California and met Ed Simmons.
Was Ed a working comedy writer at that time?**

No. He wanted to become a comedy writer,
unlike me, who wanted to become a press agent. We
were both working in the same jobs selling door to
door. We sold baby pictures. We would go up, osten-
sibly selling a free picture and then hoping to come
back with the most delicious proofs of—

**You discovered that you both were interested in
comedy?**

Right. We became friendly. Ed wanted to write,
and he was working at night writing parodies and so
forth, hoping to sell them. One night we decided to
try it together, and we wrote a parody of the Sheik of
Araby. We finished it about ten-thirty in the evening, and we went to a nightclub called the Bar of
Music, and we sold it to an entertainer for twenty-
five dollars.

That was your first sale?

That was the first sale. But that twenty-five
dollars represented about a little less than half of
what I made the previous week, and I had done it in
one evening. We did that about four times, and then
we both quit work and started to write.

How did you get together with Bud Yorkin?

Ed Simmons and I wrote a sketch called "The
Blind Date." And Jerry Lewis saw that, and he was
about to come into television. He said, "I want to
meet the writers who wrote that sketch." So Simmons and I met Jerry Lewis, and it was love at first
sight. We had only five shows left to do on the Haley
show, and when it was concluded we went to work
immediately for Dean Martin and Jerry Lewis and
started to write their very first Colgate Comedy
Hour.

Now on that Colgate Comedy Hour there were

four stage managers. One was Bud Yorkin; second was Arthur Penn; the third was John Rich; and the fourth was Jack Smythe, who all went on to become very important directors. That's where Bud and I began, on that show. Subsequently, I was to help him become director of the Martin and Lewis show when Eddie and I left it. We helped him take over the direction of the show. Then years later, after the Martha Raye show, when Ed Simmons and I split up, it was Bud Yorkin who said to me, "Why don't you come to work on the Ernie Ford show?" which he was then producing and directing. So I went to work for Bud. And then shortly after that we decided to team up.

In what ways did writing for those comedians and participating in their TV shows prepare you for the monumental task in which you are currently involved?

Just as much as living every day. Only I happen to be living at writing. But every bit of the process of living and dealing personally with all those people contributed to what I do now. Reading newspapers did. Reading a lot of Bernard Shaw did. I cut my eyeteeth on life, and I think that's what prepared me more than anything.

You mention George Bernard Shaw. Were there any other writers that you admired or patterned yourself after?

A great many that I admired. As a kid I read a lot of Shaw and Molière, and a lot of the Restoration comedies. The combination of farce and social comment always fascinated me. And from the very beginning, and this is true for anything I've ever touched, there was always something we thought we were saying. If you were to look at the Martha

Raye shows—which were stories—today, you'd find that every one of them had some social bite. All of the films I've done—look at *Cold Turkey* and *Divorce American Style*—were comments on society.

Do you feel you developed that approach as a result of steeping yourself in the plays of Molière and Shaw, because they were social critics?

I think it was certainly a help. And then, one grows up with a certain essence and feelings. I began to learn early, too, that the things that people laughed at the most were the things that they cared about the most. If you want to make people laugh, hit them where they breathe and where they live. It's much easier to get an audience to laugh after they care a lot.

There have been a great many conflicting stories on how "All in the Family" got to television. Once and for all, would you set the record straight?

I did a pilot for ABC four years before CBS said, "Let's go." I did two pilots for ABC—six months apart—they were the same show and the same casting in the lead parts—Jean Stapleton and Carroll O'Connor. We cast the young people differently each time. And the third time it was the same show, same script, and the same people in the leads. The third time was for CBS, and we went on the air.

Has the content of "All in the Family" changed any since it first went on the air?

No. That's a popular misconception, and I am right now involved in the same misconception with "Hot L Baltimore." "All in the Family" was greeted by the press as a series about a bigot. And this is a phenomenon that takes place in our country. That was the easiest thing to comment upon. The press

usually grabs the easiest thing to run with and
fastens on it. While they were fastening on the fact
that Archie Bunker would spout an occasional
racial epithet, our stories in that very first season
dealt with homosexuality, impotency, the economy,
the Nixon administration (before Watergate), the
right of privacy, and public surveillance. During
that first year, while we were treating all of those
subjects, the subject of constant talk in the press—Is
it good for the country or is it bad for the country?—
was Archie's bigotry. And when one looked at those
scripts, and many people have done that, you find
that less than five percent of almost any script was
involved with discussion of how Archie felt about
the races. The rest had to do with his attitudes, his
prejudices, toward fat people, toward homosexuals.
But it wasn't about racial bigotry.

Now, with "Hot L Baltimore," the press is
obsessed with the fact that there are two hookers
that live in the hotel and two gays who live there,
too. The show isn't about two hookers; the show isn't
about two gays; the show is about humanity and the
differences between people. And it's a kind of celebration of life, while the press talks about them
being the downtrodden and outcasts and do you
want such people in your living room? They are
people who exist in living rooms and hotels all over
the country.

**Are the people who do TV reviews capable of ana-
lyzing and critiquing the television shows?**

There are two serious failings in criticism in
this country. First of all, I think every critic should
have a strong personal philosophy from which all of
his criticism stems. And after reading a critic for a

year anybody astute enough should know this critic comes from this place philosophically. Then everything he says makes sense. You can agree with it or disagree with it. Most critics don't give you that philosophical base for a reason that I'll come to in a moment.

The second problem with most critics is they are very afraid to wear their hearts on their sleeves. The thing they find most difficult to do is to like something that is openly sentimental, because to like something that is openly sentimental is to open oneself. It is so much easier to dismiss something than it is to say "I like it. It's warm; it's human; and I like it. And these are the reasons why. . ."

That's a human failing generally, isn't it?

It could be. But both of those problems that I think the critics have prevent them from doing the same thing, and that is to open up and let the world know who they are as human beings. And that's the first obligation of the critic. This is who I am; this is my philosophical base; and everything I have to say stems from what I am.

If they were philosophically secure within themselves, would they have been able to see what "All in the Family" is about more clearly and then express it?

Yeah. "All in the Family" is a terribly sentimental show. Nobody's ever reviewed that or commented about that. Nobody has ever taken the moments when Archie has cried or Edith has had a very tender moment and written about them. Edith came home with a lump in her breast, and an audience cried and laughed at the same time. I have never read a word except from the American Cancer Society and other interested organizations. No critic ever went back to review that show, because to review that show and like it is to open oneself up.

A perfect example was the show where they go back to the hotel to celebrate their anniversary . . . very touching.

It was, and it was touching to me as many times as I saw it in rehearsal. I filled up every time when I saw it. Now, I am openly slushy. I suspect if you were to twist me hard I would gush a lot. I'm wet, and I don't mind being wet. And the American audience is wet. They love warm and tender moments, mixed with comedy, mixed with drama. The critical fraternity leadership in general in this country is loath to open itself in that way and—

They feel they might become vulnerable?

Yeah. As if fearing they might lose a sense of objectivity by joining the people and admitting, "I cried at that."

How different are the American versions of "All in the Family" and "Sanford and Son" from their English counterparts?

As different as America is from England. They are extremely different. We are now negotiating for the scripts of "All in the Family" to be produced in England under another title because they are so different from the show that it was based on.

What kind of censorship problem did you run into when "All in the Family" was first aired?

At the beginning the problems were considerably greater than they are now and have been. I didn't know I was going to be on until the very night before the show was to air, because we were still arguing about a minute and ten seconds of the show which they wanted deleted and I didn't want deleted. It wasn't until seven o'clock that I was able to call my wife and say, "Frances, we will be on tomorrow night." The fifth or sixth or seventh show of the first season was about impotency, and a section of it, not more than forty seconds, was of such concern to the network that a top executive flew out here to insist that it not be aired. But I still knew that if we didn't jump in the pool and get wet together I was going to run into this every single week.

In that particular case you did not give in to him?

In none of these cases did I. You can't get wetter than wet, and once we got wet, I would never hear from them again. And that's what happened. I did hear just occasionally in the first year and a half. And again on "Maude."

Has each of the subsequent shows presented individual problems in censorship?

The occasional show presented different problems with censorship. But I've not found myself censored. It's largely a question of dialogue, continuing dialogue, especially at CBS, because the head of the program passage at CBS is Tom Swafford. Brillant man, and insightful man. He's been an enormous help. His taste is great and so is his perception.

Have you solved each of the problems basically in the same way?

Yes. There have been times when I've simply said, "If you don't want to do the show, don't do the show, but don't ask me to do next week's show." Those times have become very rare indeed.

Do the censorship problems begin when they look over the script, or do they come down and watch a rehearsal?

We don't submit story lines, nor do we submit

scripts. We go into rehearsal. The day we go into rehearsal is the day the network gets its script. That prevents executives on any level from (a) looking at a script they may not understand and saying, "This is wrong," (b) looking at a script in which there is something they don't like that we have already changed and (c) looking at something that they hate that is going to be very different when it is performed. So for all those reasons they get a script the day we go into rehearsal. They have learned through experience not to comment on that script but to come down and see the run-through. The first comments we get are on the run-through.

Is it your intent to improve social consciousness by presenting or mirroring prejudice against and living conditions among minority groups?

I don't start anything with a presumption that I am going to succeed in changing people's minds, or raising their consciousness. I'm often asked, "What has 'All in the Family' contributed to race relations, if anything?" And my answer is, "If the Judeo-Christian ethic in several thousand years has not beaten bigotry, in this or any other country, I would be a perfect idiot to think that my little half-hour situation comedy was going to make any dents at all." I feel that about all the other things, too. I do know that when we do a show on "Good Times" about black men dying of hypertension, that within the next two weeks more black men in the country go into clinics for checkups. I know that when we do a show in which Edith comes home with a lump in her breast and talks about having found it herself, and the value of certain tests, that women all over the country will go in for the same tests.

Shouldn't that be enough to prove what a tremendous influence your shows have?

Yes, because those are specifics. When you are talking about changing attitudes, that's a nonspecific. I don't know how you'd measure that. That's where research comes in and there is all kinds of research being done on the shows, people writing doctorates on them and so forth. You can find any point of view you want.

Now what are your criteria of taste for each show?

I've got a mechanism in my belly. My belly says this is funny; my belly says this is in good taste, and this is in bad taste; and I don't know of any definition that I could possible work with.

This gut feeling—where does that come from?

Where everybody's comes from. Everybody has the same machine. I don't mean mine is different. Mine is different because I'm different, we are all different. But we all have a mechanism that tells us what's right and wrong, what is good taste and what is bad taste, what is funny and what is not funny. An artist, if he's happy, is painting what he likes, not what he thinks the next fellow will like. I write, or cause to be written, what I think is funny and what I think is tasteful.

For example, I run into trouble on toilet humor. Archie Bunker flushes it in "All in the Family." A lot of people think that's vulgar. I find nothing vulgar in it. Toilet humor makes me laugh. Mel Brooks's farting scene in *Blazing Saddles* made me laugh.

I think America has lost a good deal of its sense of humor in the last twenty years. We used to pride ourselves on being able to kid ourselves a great deal, but now I think that is just something that Bob Hope alludes to now and then, and the reality of it is horseshit.

We don't laugh at ourselves really as much as we used to when there was a Will Rogers and the times were easier. We are a little more self-conscious, and we've lost sight of that wonderful American ability to laugh at ourselves. And when we had that, there was a Chick Sale, and all of his humor was bathroom humor, and I loved it; I loved the bawdy.

It seems to me that the very first joke or bit of amusement that passes between a parent and a child is a toilet joke. It has something to do with "doodoo" or "ahah" or "peepee" or something of that nature. And it's perfectly lovely. That innocent, dear little joke about the human anatomy and its functions that passes between a parent and a child, it's absolutely lovely.

It never grew less lovely to me as I grew older. And so I roar at that kind of joke and I think America will, and America does indeed. It is the think tank, in the form of critics here or senators there, or FCC chairmen there, who say for the rest of America, "That is naughty." They are saying that is naughty while America is laughing.

Is there any . ubject that cannot be done today that you feel you will want to do someday?

I can't think of any, or any that I would want to do. There are those subjects perhaps that I might not wish to do.

What kind of problems, in terms of story content and character development, do you encounter with each show?

Well, what I am resisting in the question is the

designation of the problem as *mine*. The problem isn't mine. As we work closer together, the various writers and I, the problem is *ours*. They feel as strongly about the things I feel as I feel myself. So when there's a problem in the story, I may be the one to point it out, but everybody is there to solve it or help solve it. Or maybe somebody else is pointing it out. But it becomes our problem, and we are all reaching toward the same goal. I may be the one because it's my own peculiar madness to suggest that somebody dies at the end of the first act of a "Maude" episode. I may find a little bit of resistance. How can you be funny and have somebody drop dead? Because you can. Because death isn't altogether unfunny. And we can work it somehow. It's just going to take a little time. That's a case in point. It actually happened. But the next time another idea came up that seemed a little outrageous, it was no longer a consideration that it couldn't be done; it just became a question of how hard do we have to work to find the answer.

Is there any one specific attitude that pervades all of your shows?

If there is a specific attitude it would be this intention: that every show be a celebration of life. We try to do shows where people cheer, where people yell, where they fight hard, they bed a lot.

Everybody is feeling and everybody is caring, and everybody is living at the top of his vitality whatever the crisis is in the individual story. To me it's all a celebration of life, and everything to me is positive because that's the way I feel about life. I like waking up each day. I would hope—at least that's the intention—that people turn off these shows and feel better for having seen them.

Then each one of them has a Norman Lear stamp, your philosophy of life, the joy of living?

Well, that's a more presumptuous way than I would put it. It is, it goes with the territory. This book you're preparing is going to have your stamp—the way you put it together is going to reflect the way you feel about it. The way we put shows together is the reflection that begins with me but doesn't end there, and that's a very important point. There are a lot of people that contribute to the success of these shows, not the least of which are the actors, let alone the writers and directors. So it's a great combination and collaboration. There is no doubt that I spark it—that's what I'm here for—but everybody contributes to the effort.

A lot of the laughter that comes from Archie grows out of his use of malaprops and bizarre nicknames. Do the comic lines come easier when writing a family episode because of this character with built-in humor?

Yeah. All of the attitudes have become staples. They are helpful. Anybody who sits down to write "All in the Family" for the first time has many things going for him. The minute Archie walks into the kitchen and sees Mike at the refrigerator is a laugh. Any reference to Mike eating is an automatic laugh. If Archie misuses a word, the public is accustomed to it. Of course they'll laugh. If you weren't on every week, you'd never have those aids, but they are tools.

When the writers submit an idea or story line, what do you look for, aside from humor?

A good, solid piece of substance, something that is substantial, that an actor can bite into, and that has something more important to it than just a series of one-line jokes.

Then the subject matter would be very important?
Very important, yes. Somebody comes in and says, "How about a mentally retarded kid who falls in love with Gloria?" That's at once sweet and poignant. But Archie's attitude toward the mentally retarded can be made very amusing, and Mike's fight with him about it even more amusing. One of the better shows we've done was on that subject.
In what way do you feel your shows get away from the standard situation comedy series?
All the forerunners of "All in the Family" dealt with lost skate keys and roasts that were ruined while the boss was coming to dinner. And I never saw anything wrong with that. It's just my preference. If I'm going to be doing it, I'll work with substance. Parenthetically, the people have said accusingly, "Why do you express strong points of view in situation comedy? That's no forum for social comment and points of view." Well, situation comedy is not a label that I accept. That's what it's called, I know, but I consider I'm doing a half hour of theater, and my genre is comedy.
I also feel that given ten years, or more, of situation comedies with nothing more important than a bowling ball being lost, or a wife who dented a fender and the husband mustn't find out—often years of shows that conveyed a very definite point of view, but in a negative way, by indifference, even—
They never faced up to the real problems.
Yeah, they were saying there was no Viet Nam, there was no race problem, there were no race riots, there was nothing wrong with the economy. By never facing up to anything they were presenting the picture with a very definite point of view: All's right with the world. But all isn't right with the world, and it seems to me that one point of view is

just as strong as the other and no stronger. Everything we're doing is no stronger than anything that was done preceding it. It's just different.

All your shows are filmed live with an audience. What's the difference in doing this rather than filming a show over a three-day period?

The difference is theater—what we were talking about. Our shows are a theatrical experience. They are taped before a live audience, and that's why in a taped show with a live audience actors are seen to pause. Now and then there is still a letter asking, "Why is he looking into the camera?" He's not looking into the camera; he's waiting for the laugh to stop. "Is he reading cue cards?" He's not reading cue cards; he's waiting for the laughter to cease. The acting is timed like it would be timed in the theater.

That's one of the advantages. Are there any others?

That's the biggest advantage. We all love theater. And that's why ninety percent of the people who work on these shows are from the stage.

I've noticed that it also lends a spontaneity that you get, which is the essence—

Which is the theater. It's happening now.

The credits on each of your shows indicate that several writers are involved in the writing of each episode. Why is it necessary to have so many people working on one show?

Because nothing is written, it's rewritten. I think that was first said by George Kaufman. And it's quite true. And the average writer doesn't have the time to spend. We spend months and months and months on some scripts. Nobody's paid enough to do that, so it's only our team who can afford to do that. So two writers may write it from the outside. The second draft is done by two writers on the inside, and the third draft and a fourth and a fifth and a sixth by all the guys on the inside, and that's how a dozen writers' names may appear on a credit.

Some comedy writers have a reputation for being good sketch writers, and others are considered to be good situation writers. What's the difference?

I don't know. I think a good writer is a good writer is a good writer. Talent is at a premium anywhere. There are very few good violinists—everybody else plays the fiddle—and the same is true of writers. There are very few good writers. Everybody else fiddles around. A good writer will write a good joke and know something about construction, too.

There was an article in *Newsweek* that stated, "Topnotch comedy writers were in such short supply that some commanded as much as seven thousand dollars a week." Why is there such a shortage of good writers?

I think the answer is what I was just saying. Talent. If you are looking for a good orthopedic surgeon, you're not going to get that many great recommendations. There just is a limit to the amount of talent. I think it's right that it be so, because if everybody had talent it wouldn't be precious at all.

In a recent *People* magazine story, you said, "All art tends to be autobiographical, even television." Would you explain what you meant by that?

Well, we all write largely out of our own experience on these shows anyway. That's what I meant by that. We're constantly dredging up memories of something that happened yesterday. We talked to our kids; we listened to our wives; we read the newspapers. And an awful lot of what we do comes right out of what we're living.

In the many quotes attributed to you regarding your

attitude toward comedy, you say that it has to be "honest" and "real." What exactly do those words have to do with making people laugh?

People laugh the hardest, I find, at things they care about, and the things they care about are real things. When Edith goes, as she did in one show, to a wedding without Archie and runs into a cousin that she used to love when she was a little girl, and is feeling the same way toward him, and learns in the middle of the scene that he is not a cousin, she is suddenly all aflutter. This man she has been feeling this way about is not even a relative, and as she's starting to feel that guilt, the audience is caring enormously for the situation and predicament she is in, and they are laughing twice as hard. So the reality and the honesty work to advantage in that sense.

An article in the *Los Angeles Times* said that your taste in comedy has "always tended toward *ideas* rather than *manners* or *broad slapstick.*" What's the difference between those two?

Well, I've told you why I feel substance is important to me. But I adore slapstick. But nothing I'm doing do I care to watch as much as I would care to watch Laurel and Hardy pictures, for example, or Buster Keaton. I would much rather watch them than what I do. But I would much rather do what I'm doing.

In a *Newsweek* article about TV comedy you were quoted as saying, "The guy who comes home from work wants to be entertained, but not with pap. He'll laugh at his own problems if they are mirrored for him." What did you mean?

Well, I was talking about the age-old adage, which I think is bullshit, that the average American male wants to be entertained, that he doesn't want to be faced with his problems when he comes home, that when he goes to the theater all he wants is dancing girls. And I think "All in the Family" and the other shows indicate what I think about that. Because we face the average American with his problems all the time. True, we do it in comedy, but everything should entertain, be it drama or comedy. Drama should make you care and cry, and comedy should make you groan with laughter. But we certainly face up to the problems, and the public loves it. There again is that think-tank philosophy which says that the average American has a mentality of thirteen, another crock.

Let's say there was a talented but unknown young writer somewhere in America who wanted to write a segment for one of your shows. How would he go about it?

He'd have a hell of a time, because they come in by the hundreds; they can't be read—

The scripts, you mean?

Yeah. And ideas, and whatnot. First of all for legal reasons they can't even be opened. Nine hundred people have the same idea at the same moment, and one of them makes it to the air, and you've got eighty lawsuits. So you can't even get them open. If I were living anywhere in the country and wanted to write for television, I'd come to California. There is no way you can be in this town working at getting read and not get read.

Through perseverance?

Yes, absolutely. You come to this office, for example, and see that young woman sitting out front and tell her you have something for Norman Lear to read and just do it six times and be agreeable, and Jadie Jo is going to start to know you and like you, and before you know it she's forcing me to read something. It's just in the nature of things.

So that if someone wants to write and take the pains, he will be read, sooner or later?

Yeah. But he needs to get off his duff and get where the action is.

Time **magazine once described comedy writers as having "a congenital air of melancholy." What is it about the field of comedy that seems to attract people with these particular emotional characteristics?**

Well, a lot of comedy writers have come out of the ghetto—one ghetto or another. That's where one sharpens one's sense of humor on just the things we've been talking about, the hardships and realities of life and the conflicts of living under those hardships. So coming out of that maybe gives a lot of people a sense of melancholy but a great sense of humor. An outward appearance of melancholy and a great inner drive and sense of humor. For me, personally, if there's anybody having a better time on the North American continent you have to show me who it is. I have a great time. I laugh ninety percent of every day with the greatest people in the world, and when I'm not doing that I'm thinking about it. So I don't know how to say I'm having a bad time.

Mel Brooks talked about being in psychoanalysis, and I know that you're also a great believer. Is there some secret ingredient that a psychiatrist can provide a comedy writer that will help him in his work?

If there is any ingredient, if any psychiatrist has it, he wouldn't be a psychiatrist tomorrow; he would be a manufacturer of the ingredient. I don't think he supplies the comedy writer anything he doesn't supply anybody else—for anybody who hasn't found his own freedom, hasn't been able to learn to appreciate himself. Psychiatry and religion, when they work, both function in the same way. Religion is psychiatry once removed. I love God, and God loves me, therefore I love myself. Psychiatry discards the first two steps, goes straight to the point. I love myself. Psychiatry can't do anything but help any artist, or any human being, simply by helping him become freer to express himself. I wouldn't divorce the comedy writer from the rest of society that cares about psychiatry.

But aren't comedy writers different from other people?

No.

You don't think so?

I don't think so.

More sensitive, more aware?

Well, creative people generally might be a little more sensitive, but I'm constantly amazed how creative a lot of people are who aren't in creative fields. I sometimes think that we in the so-called arts think we have a lock on sensitivity and creativity. And hell, a guy comes to the house to paint a fence, and when you talk to him and you watch him work, you suddenly realize that he, in his own way, is as creative and sensitive as anybody you're working with in the so-called arts. We don't have a lock on it.

The executive producer of "Maude," Rod Parker, has referred to you as a "spiritual leader who can still write a very funny joke." Is this a good example of having that strong foundation as a comedy writer way back in the beginning?

Oh, there is no way I could do what I do if I wasn't a writer. There'd be no reason for the Rod Parkers of my life to listen to me if I wasn't also a writer.

"Good Times" producer Allan Manings says that you are aware of all versions of all scripts and have made suggestions on each of them. What kind of ability is required to be so conscientiously involved in so many projects?

I don't know. It's a question of love. I love them. It's probably as simple as that. I love the shows; I love the projects; I love all of those writers and directors. I mean, you just mentioned two sensational guys. It's wonderful to be with them, and I have a ball doing it. The answer is that. I simply like it.

You now have more shows on the air than any other independent producer in the history of television. Where do you go from here?

We are preparing more shows, because there are lots of other areas. If we're not typecast, we have to come out with a couple of shows with a very different format from the ones we're doing.

Are there any challenges, any goals you are still striving for?

Sure, lots of them. If I thought that I had done what there was to be done, for me as an individual, a lot of things would be over for me instead of just beginning. I'm still the slushy fool who believes that tomorrow's the first day of the rest of my life. And tomorrow is the first day of the rest of my thinking, too.

Carl
REINER

C arl Reiner was born March 20, 1922, in the Bronx, the son of a watchmaker. As a teenager he enrolled in a drama school and later landed a part in a small theater group's rendition of *The Merry Widow*. (This segment of his life was portrayed by Reni Santori in the film version of Reiner's novel, *Enter Laughing*.)

While serving as a radio operator with the Signal Corps during World War II, Reiner was assigned to a Special Services unit where Howard Morris was his first sergeant. He also met Sid Caesar there, and the threesome toured the Pacific for eighteen months in G.I. revues. Reiner earned the first two of his eleven Emmy Awards when the group reunited later on television for "Your Show of Shows."

Out of the army in 1946, Reiner won the leading role in a road company production of *Call Me Mister*, which he later repeated on Broadway.

His talent for writing comedy began to emerge with the publication of *Enter Laughing*, several shows for Dinah Shore, and the screenplay for *The Thrill of It All,* starring James Garner and Doris Day.

Reiner's other motion picture credits include:
The Art of Love (screenplay)
Where's Poppa? (director)
The Comic (producer, director, and co-writer with Aaron Ruben)
Enter Laughing (director)
Reiner also wrote and directed the Broadway play *Something Different* and has made four hit comedy albums with his close friend Mel Brooks:
The 2000-Year-Old Man
The 2001-Year-Old Man
Carl Reiner and Mel Brooks at the Cannes Film Festival
The 2000-Year-Old Man Is Now 2000 and Thirteen
Reiner created and subsequently became producer of "The New Dick Van Dyke Show," and as creator-writer-producer of "The Dick Van Dyke Show" received a total of seven more Emmy Awards.

Carl married the former Estelle Lebost in 1943. They have three children, Ann, Lucas, and Rob, who has emerged as a sensitive comedy actor in his own right on the award-winning television show "All in the Family."

Carl Reiner—writer, actor, comedian, director, producer, novelist, TV moderator, recording star, and winner of eleven Emmy Awards—is still building up credits. He is now executive producer of and acting in the ABC comedy series, "Good Heavens."

This interview took place in Carl Reiner's beautiful Beverly Hills home on the hottest day in the history of Los Angeles. Carl wore sandals and a blue short-sleeved sport shirt and light blue striped pants. The living room was attractive and tastefully decorated, with many abstract paintings lining the walls.

Carl Reiner is an unpretentious man. Confident, expressive, and rather serious, he spoke without hesitation, offering his opinions directly and with great assurance.

When we finished talking I was treated to a 100 percent genuine New York egg cream.

Carl Reiner the actor came before Carl Reiner the comedy writer.

Oh, yes. Way before!

What were the motivating factors that led you to begin writing comedy?

It was having an interest in making people laugh—even when I was very young. I think you are a writer long before you know you're a writer. In my case it was the Sid Caesar show that brought it out. I sat in a room full of writers.

I had always written material for myself. In the army I started doing comedy, and I started collecting material. When you're very young you're influenced by certain shows and comedians. You steal; you paste together pieces. But in the army I started writing a couple of totally original things. I realized then I could write, at least little sketches and jokes. Then when I worked with Sid Caesar—I was hired as an actor. One day I came in with a concept for a sketch, and Max Liebman, the producer, said, "Let Carl sit in the writers' room." That was after the third week I'd been on the show.

As a performer.

Yes. But for the rest of the nine years I was with Sid and Max—Sid for four, Max for five—I sat in the writers' room during the week and we rehearsed only after we'd written the material in concert. I was without portfolio. I didn't have a credit as a writer, but I was a *talking* writer the way most of them were. Only one fellow sat at the typewriter. The rest of us talked, and the selector—was Sid actually—and the major fellow at the typewriter. That started it for me. **Then it was smooth sailing from then on?**

No. Then came a whole period of denigration by the other writers. When we'd have an argument about what's funny, what's usable, they'd say, "What the hell do you know about writing? You're only an actor!"

Then everybody on the staff was always saying, "When I write my book, when I write my book." So one summer—I just wanted to see if I could write without the help of the other writers—I wrote a book called *Enter Laughing*. I had written some short stories the year before, just to learn how to type, actually, and a friend of mine handed them to an editor at Simon and Schuster. And he said, "Hey, this is very good stuff!" And he asked me to write a book. I said, "What about the short stories?" He said, "Any one of these stories could become a book if you expand it." So I started *Enter Laughing*.

It was really because I was being frustrated by the writers on the show. Sometimes you have collaborators when you don't need them. You say, "It's a Thursday morning, and he's walking down the street," and the collaborator says, "Friday is funnier. Make it Friday morning." Sometimes you can use a collaborator, and other times it's just somebody else's ego or vanity rather than your own.

During the formative stages of your writing career, were there any signposts that helped direct you toward a particular area of comedy?

I don't know about signposts, but *influences*— the people you admired, the things that made you

laugh. The Marx Brothers made me laugh. They always had a crazy story that they hung everything onto. It was nonsensical comedy with a sort of thread through it. I think I was influenced by them.
The Marx Brothers *pictures?*

Pictures, yes. As a kid, I thought Chaplin was a genius. You know, as we grow older, we find some funny people we had bypassed. Maybe bacause of our age and the time they hit. Like Buster Keaton. I never realized how funny he was until I started researching him for a movie I was doing. I was also influenced by Eddie Cantor, who I thought made great movies. What's great when you're twelve or thirteen doesn't always remain great in your opinion.

Some of Cantor's radio programs—the scripts, the material he used was very well done.

Very, and he influenced me an awful lot. He was one of my favorites at a certain age. When I got older I realized he lacked a certain sophistication.

He did everything right on the nose.

Yeah, right on the nose.

But that's the audience he was playing to.

Yeah, right. And when you're ten or twelve years old, on the nose is perfect.

You once said in an interview with columnist Sidney Fields that the Sid Caesar show was your "writing college." In what way did that show help you develop your writing craft?

Sitting in a room with some very brilliant writers. There may have been a dozen that came through those office halls. Some stayed a year, some two. "Doc" Simon, Mel Brooks, Mel Tolkin, Tony Webster, Joe Stein. Their credits were something to contend with. From *Fiddler on the Roof* to all of Neil Simon's work.

Sitting in a room with those guys for nine years and hearing opinions about what's funny and what's not. Hearing a man make a joke. Mel Brooks, of course—maybe one of the biggest influences on my life. He's the man who I think is the single most funny human being in the world today. He makes me laugh. And watching his mind at work and examining it while it's working. Each man has techniques even though he may not be aware they're techniques.

Then you absorbed the craft of writing by osmosis.

No, not by osmosis, by intuition. I think the craft of writing is intuitive. If you're somebody who walks through life *naturally* examining things— which is what I always did. My father was an inventor, and he was always aware of how things were put together. So you become aware, for example, why certain pieces of drama work.

Nobody taught me. Nobody sat me down and said, "Hey, to have a good scene here, you have to build this . . ." I'm not aware of it. I go by the seat of my pants.

Because you loved Eddie Cantor and the other comedians of his era, is it possible that you absorbed their techniques into your unconscious . . .

Oh, of course.

. . . And then later it erupted and came from your brain to your hand?

I think so. I think every *thing,* every experience you have in life mulches into a total being. Seeing good drama, being affected by good drama. Being an actor, too. As a young man, I acted in an awful lot of plays in summer stock. Summer theaters usually do plays that have been successful. They were successful because they told a story; they had dramatic

moments; they had conflict. And you *feel* them. I
write that way. I write by saying, "Hey, at this
moment I think we should get a little interest or a
little mystery or a little excitement going here."
**Is it possible to describe the mental process in
creating a joke? That is, can you break it down into
steps?**
I wouldn't even try. I find the best jokes arise
from natural conversations, realities that veer off
from the expected. If you have somebody say, "Good
morning," and the other guy says, "You're full of
shit," that's not an answer. It's unexpected and you
might laugh at it. That's not a joke, particularly.

When people have normal conversations and
somebody says the untoward, sometimes the very
honest reaction, the absolute truth is the thing that
makes people laugh. Most people do not say exactly
what they feel, because society demands that a
certain amount of politeness exist. But the comedian says exactly what he feels. Groucho Marx was
a prime example of that. He'd say, "Hey, lady, you're
fat." or "You're standing on my foot." He'd go to the
absolute truth. There was nothing really surprising
about it except that the man would say what everybody was already thinking. The comedian says it. I
don't know how to break down a joke. That's a tough
one. Max Eastman could probably do it for you.
**In a *Newsday* interview you said, "Anybody who
writes anything is writing autobiography. Including murder mysteries." Would you explain that?**
I don't mean that in a murder mystery people
who write them have murdered. But they can pull
from within themselves the *feeling* of wanting to
murder and what it would be like to murder. Everybody has the potential to kill in him. Most of it is

suppressed to the point where we don't even know it's there. A writer tries everything on for size—good writers do. Good writers, when they write about cowardice, they are writing about the moments in their lives that were fearful or cowardly. When they're writing about heroism, they're writing about those moments, too. When they're writing about murder, they're writing about moments they felt like murdering somebody and how it might be.

I think that statement holds true for the writers who are of the first magnitude. Writers who move you when you read them are writers who are working from their own experiences, even though when a writer writes about a woman and he's not a woman, he can only guess. When a woman is crying, he has to cry for her.

Have the compassion—

Yeah, but I think basically all people are the same, men and women. I don't think a man can get into a woman's psyche. It may seem that he's done that. Somebody said that the female problem in the world is that most of the propaganda written about how women feel was written by men. Most of the great novels, the heroines—

That's true. There's a certain amount of writing that has to be put down when you're preparing a script or writing jokes. What about the improvisational comedy that you and Mel Brooks did for the record albums?

That's the same thing as writing. It's just *talking*—writing. All writers ad-lib. When somebody says, "It's better because it's improvised"— every piece of creative writing is improvised. Where does it come from, when it comes? So you put it on paper. Mel and I were performing writers in that situation, when we sit in front of a microphone and ad-lib. A lot of it's bad; a lot of it fails—just the way you scratch out a thing on a piece of paper.

We edited the tapes the way an editor of a publishing house might edit a writing piece. Just take out lines by blue-penciling them. We did it with the scissors. Improvisation is just writing in front of an audience. Allowing them to see the creative process and allowing them to see your failures along with your successes. A writer when he writes something doesn't allow you to see his failures. He scratches it out, tears it up, burns it.

And we get the best results of it.

Yeah. We get the synthesis of all the bad stuff. So improvisation is no more than writing with your mouth.

Comedian Morey Amsterdam once said of you, "He's a genius—he's the only ad-lib comedy writer I know. He can write funny on his feet." Do you feel you do your best work this way, or would you rather be at your desk with plenty of time at your disposal?

I work both ways. Because I was a performer, I do enjoy an audience laughing. Morey was talking about the old Dick Van Dyke show, and the new one worked the same way. I do best in rewrites when there's an audience around, when we're sitting around a table. At that point, you've tried the original words on for size, and they don't make the joke or make people laugh as much as you want, so you continue from there.

Having the advantage of being a performer, I can get up and show how it might look, how it might be funny. But you don't get any more credit for one or the other. It depends on the final material. How you arrived at it doesn't matter, whether you typed it or dictated it.

The end result is what counts.

That's right!

What effect does a writer's ethnic background have on his approach to comedy?

Vive la ethnic difference! It has been said and it probably is true that a certain amount of suffering is necessary to hone a comedy mind. Deprivation, poverty. We haven't found indications of many comedians coming from an affluent background.

London Lee grew up in wealthy surroundings, but I've always felt that he was deprived.

Yes, but in a different way.

Deprived of love, perhaps.

Or something. And the fact that he wanted to be a comedian even though he was rich. Swimming upstream might have honed him that way. We don't know what his other problems were. Maybe he did have love. Having experiences of the sad nature, the deprived background seems to hone comedians. W. C. Fields, Chaplin.

Are you saying then that the exact same environmental conditions motivate the comedy writer?

Oh, I think so. The comedy writer performs with his pencil instead of his voice. He's still thrashing out at society, making fun of society, saying terrible things about society. It's a kick in the pants no matter how you look at it. Most comedy writers usually attack society. Something structured, something bigger than they are. They don't pick on poor people. They go after kings.

All writers have a method of working: specific hours for writing, the kind of atmosphere they feel

comfortable in, et cetera. What are your writing habits?

I do best in the morning. I start at eight or nine and go till three or four o'clock at the typewriter. Some people work best at night. It's individual. I don't think it matters much when you do it or how you do it.

Do you have a specific place to work?

I wrote *Enter Laughing* in a room on Fire Island. I kept the typewriter on my lap. I wrote a lot of Van Dyke shows upstairs here in a little den. I write in the office where we produced the show. You can write anywhere if you get a good idea.

You were supposed to have written *Enter Laughing* by working four hours a day, seven days a week, for five weeks.

It was more than four hours a day. It was actually about five or six. I gave myself a schedule. I said, "It's going to be about 250 or 300 pages. If I do five pages a day, I'll have it done by September." And I did it that way. I never got away from the typewriter unless I did an average of five pages a day. Some days four, some days six, when I'd come to the end of a point or thought or scene or something.

How about rewriting?

Some of it I did as I went along. I got some awfully good ideas in the middle, and I went back and started again.

Then when you say "five pages a day" you mean five pages that were written, rewritten, and polished.

Yeah. Before I'd write those five pages, what I'd do is read the last couple of chapters. Sometimes I'd read from the beginning, to get a flow going, get myself cooked and juiced up again—primed—and then go another five pages, and then the next day I'd read up to that point and go forward again. Some days I'd go into town to do some panel shows. So the next day I'd do twelve pages to make up for it.

Do you feel a greater degree of self-discipline is necessary when you tackle a substantial project like a novel?

I think the greatest self-discipline is when you're doing something that isn't on order, something for yourself, something you have to write and you're not absolutely sure it will be bought. If you get an assignment for television, there is no discipline. It's just fear. You're afraid you won't get the material in time for the actors to put in on the camera.

When you're doing a novel, self-discipline is important, but a deadline is even more important. I said to the publisher, "Give me a date when you want this." He didn't care if he got it in October or December or next May. So he said arbitrarily, "September." I said, "Good. Now I have a date to work for." You'll find that most writers need that. Mozart worked that way.

You had comparatively little difficulty selling *Enter Laughing.*

It was my original intent to publish some short stories, call it *A Penny Apiece,* and have thirty-five short stories for thirty-five cents in a pocket book. Well, this editor named Goodwin at Simon and Schuster said, "Short stories don't sell, but this material suggests you could write a novel."

I said, "I don't know how to write a novel."

He said, "Just take any one of these you like and write everything you know about it. Everything you can think about it." So I picked up one of the short stories and expanded it. I should look back at the other stories. Maybe I'll have twelve other novels.

Then *Enter Laughing* **was written by the seat of your pants, so to speak—by trial and error?**

Yeah. I started to tell a saga of a young boy. I didn't know where I was going. Actually, I wanted to tell the story of an actor—myself—from the time I started till the present day, and I never got past a three-day period. The book encompassed a three-day period in a kid's life.

I only have the pocket book edition but that represented three hundred *typewritten* **pages?**

Oh, it must've been over three hundred. It came out to about two hundred and forty printed pages.

While working on it did you take it to the editor often for suggestions or improvements?

No. I wrote the first eighteen pages, and I remember I didn't know what I was writing or what I was doing. I got a call from the editor, and he said, "How's it going?"

I said, "I got eighteen pages."

He said, "Send them along."

I said, "I'm glad, because I don't know if it's right or what."

And when he read them he said, "Just keep going. You're on your way!" I never contacted him again until I finished the novel.

There's an interesting dramatic part to this story. I finished it a month early, and I was so excited I called Simon and Schuster and asked to speak to Mr. Goodwin. They said, "Mr. Goodwin died yesterday." A real shock. He was the only contact I had with the firm. And he had died, a forty-eight-year-old man. He was the only one who knew I was writing it. He gave me the deal. So I put the novel in the drawer and I said, "That's it!" About a month later, I got a call from Lee Wright, a woman, a brilliant editor, and she came out and read the book and edited it with me.

What percentage of comedy writing is craft and what percent art?

[*Laughing*] What kind of comedy writing are you talking about? The excellent, the sensational comedy writing is one hundred percent art. The rotten stuff is one hundred percent craft. I don't know. That's a tough one. I've never really thought about that. The inspired comedy, the comedy that comes out of people because they have to be funny is mostly art.

All writing can't be inspired.

Yeah. All comedy writers can't always be inspired, but if comedy writers aren't inspired, then they're not comedy writers. Then they're people who have *guessed* at how comedy is put together and are working at it. There are people, the originators of comedy, guys who have an original bent, your real creative comedians, they think funny, they are funny. But they've all learned craft.

There's a theory that writers produce work out of their subconscious, using that part of the mind to organize ideas and to solve whatever writing problems come about. How do you feel about this theory?

Intuition is a better word than *subconscious*. You use every part of you when you write, but sometimes things pop into your head or pop on the typewriter, and you're not aware you're thinking them. Harold Pinter said, "When you're writing, if a character walks onto your paper and says more than five lines it's hard to get rid of him." I think that's a marvelous theory, and I've found it is absolutely true.

Has it worked for you?

Oh, yes. In writing *Something Different,* I had an exterminator delivering cockroaches. I had written him for one joke. It started out as an off-stage, one-sided conversation. I had my main character trying to re-create a room in which he had written his first novel and now he was trying to write another one. Something was missing. He found that the cockroaches were missing. So he called up an exterminator and has this one-sided conversation. Which is really why I wrote it.

When the exterminator delivered the cockroaches, he was so funny as he kept talking that he became the cathartic in the play. He became the third central character, as important as the other two characters. I couldn't get him out of the room. He kept talking. He was funny. When I read what Pinter said, I said, "Hey, that's true. That's what happens."

How important is the reading of joke books or humorous novels and stories in the comedy writer's development?

When they're very young it's very important. If they continue to do that, then they're not comedy writers. They're guys who appreciate jokes. They're collectors, anthologists. We all did that as kids. I'm not that creative a joke writer. I haven't made many great jokes in my life that I could put my finger on. I write good character comedy. My characters say funny things, but I can't write a good joke, the kind you read in a book. I don't know where they come from. Whoever invents those are geniuses. All people who are interested in comedy read those things and are influenced by them.

Does knowing English grammar or having a large vocabulary help a writer create funny lines?

Well, it depends on who you're writing for and what you're writing. Certain things are impossible to write without a vocabulary. I was always intimidated by the fact that I had a meager vocabulary. I thought erudition was important—to be a writer you had to be erudite. My wife pointed out to me once that it was more important to *touch people's feelings*. It doesn't matter how you touch people. It's more likely you'll touch people with simple words because they'll understand you. Most people who want to be understood are trying to make a point.

Philosophers, scientists, politicians, political science writers—the ones who are good write very simply. They have interest in your learning or seeing their point. The use of big words sometimes is a subterfuge to hide what you're saying or the fact that you don't have too much to say.

William A. Buckley is a perfect example of that. He'd rather use a big word than make himself clear. He's never very clear. He sounds like he's clear, but he's not. You see him every once in a while with people who have language at their disposal—with much greater skill than Buckley's. They don't use it. They'll use it to point out what he's doing. I don't know why I picked on Buckley, but he's a prime example of a guy with a lot of language, and he doesn't touch you. Hemingway used very simple language.

Sheldon Leonard, the producer, has been quoted as saying that you have "one of the finest instincts for comedy of anybody in the business." Is that instinct a natural talent, or is it something anyone can develop?

Gee, I don't know. I think it's natural *and* deve-loped. You start with it naturally, and then you develop it. As you get applauded for something you do instinctively, you keep doing it, and it develops by usage. It's just like swimming. Everybody can swim naturally, and the more you swim, the better you are at it.

A lot of people don't swim or can't swim because they're afraid of the water.

Yeah, but that's something else. I mean it's a natural thing to learn. To keep your breath, to float. You play with a kid in the water and he'll learn to swim. You don't have to teach them anything. Then when they want to go faster, they'll learn how to—

But when you say instinctively—you grew up in New York—

But I grew up making jokes and making people laugh and doing funny things.

Why?

That's instinct! Self-preservation, too. It's a tool. By the way, it enabled me to be hostile without getting hit. Make people laugh. The court jester is the best example of that. He told the king he was full of shit. But he told him in such a charming, cute way. He made a cute little face after it and did a somer-sault, and he'd say, "I'm only kidding." He could say the most outlandish things. "Methinks the king is growing fat. Ah, but fat, sire, is a thing that makes most people . . ." and he'd make some beautiful poetic analogy or something and get away with it.

Do you ever get writing blocks? And if so, how do you overcome them?

When you write and you have a deadline and you have a writing block, you chop the block down by just sitting at a typewriter. But there are times when you have nothing on order, nothing pressing, and it becomes— I don't call it a block; I call it laziness. Right now I don't feel like writing. I haven't written anything since *Something Different*. Oh, no; I wrote a picture with Aaron Rubin, *The Comic*. That was the last thing. Then I wrote the new Van Dyke pilot. But not really concentrated writing like when I did the first Dick Van Dyke show. I did twenty-two scripts one year, twenty the next year, and last year I did four scripts for the show.

While *Something Different* was trying out in Boston I happened to be appearing at a nightclub and I saw the show at a Wednesday matinee. I noticed you sitting in the back with a secretary. Were you giving her notes as the director or the writer?

Both—because I was the director—writer of the play. So if I wanted a line changed, I'd have her make a note of that. Sometimes it was a directorial note on staging, or one of the actors was doing something wrong.

Is it an advantage to be both the director and the author?

I know about the *dis*advantages. The advantages I'm not sure of. It's very hard. In a theater situation the writer needs time to do the repairs, and he usually does them at night. And then you hand the script changes to the director, who gives them to the actors the next morning—while the writer sleeps. But it's very difficult when you're doing both. I did a massive amount of rewrites on that play, really massive. I don't know how I did it.

There's a chapter in Bill Goldwin's book, *The Season,* about *Something Different*. He saw the play about five times—from its inception. All the rehearsals, all the dress rehearsals, out-of-town tryouts, the opening on Broadway, and he knew it very well. He was amazed at one man being able to do all the work without getting rattled. In his book, he talks about the fact that one time my tongue was on fire. I went to a mirror on the way out of the room and I said, "Hey, what's wrong with my tongue? It's burning!" Like I had a vitamin deficiency. I never found out what it was. But you pay a toll for all that work.

Would you do it again?

I don't know. If I did another play, I'd have somebody direct who directs better than I.

What percentage of the original script is changed during the tryouts from its conception until it opens on Broadway?

I would say about ninety-five percent.

From the original script?

The way I did it, yes. I don't mean that the story changed. In my case, I don't think there was one line left alone. I changed something about every line. Maybe I'm wrong; maybe it's seventy-five or eighty percent, but—

But it's the majority?

Oh, yes. There are certain things that remain intact because they were perfect. But then you start with actors, and you're creative, and you're director-writer. You see the actors do something, and you start writing right on your feet. You say, "Hey, you say this and you say that."

Now here is a case where a producer bought your play and several weeks or months later he saw seventy-five percent change from the script he had already been satisfied with.

A producer is never terribly satisfied. Well, they are to some degree, but most of them think there are rewrites to be done. And they are aware that there are going to be a lot of rewrites done. Tennessee Williams writes two or three complete plays while out of town, I understand. He just keeps writing. I threw out a whole act and never replaced it.

During the break-in period, what percentage of the laughs come as a result of rewriting?

Oh, I don't know; that's a tough question. I know that every time you do a rewrite *to* get a laugh and you *don't* get a laugh, you keep rewriting until you *do* get a laugh. If you feel you need one there.

Do the actors contribute any of the laughs?

Oh, boy—and how.

Any way to estimate how much of the total?

I don't know what percentage. That's a hard thing to judge. But I would say that any time I've ever done anything I've been fortunate—in fact, insistent—in getting what I call *players* rather than *actors*. People who are creative, who can play with the material. I've always had that. From the time I was with Sid Caesar, who's an incredibly creative comedian, to Dick Van Dyke. When I gave him something to do I thought was funny, he made it hilarious. And in *Something Different* I had really creative actors on stage. They gave me dozens and dozens and dozens of laughs that were not in the original script, just by their behavior, by their attitude and sometimes even lines.

In a *TV Guide* article about "The Dick Van Dyke Show" you said, "I like to do warm zany comedy. Big crazy humor played by real people. Warm is an important word. You laugh easier when funny things are happening to nice people." Isn't that a rather unorthodox view, since most experts feel comedy must always have a target or criticize the fabric of society?

Actually, that quote wasn't mine. Somebody said that about my work. I wrote a thing called *Thrill of It All,* and they said, "Carl Reiner, he writes warm, zany things." Which is a strange combination—to be warm and zany at the same time. I wasn't aware that I was doing that. Somebody labeled that, and it stuck in my mind, and it came out during that interview.

At that time we were doing situation comedy, and in situation comedy you have to like the *foreground*—the people; otherwise, you won't buy the premise. Lucy is great. Whatever she does is great because you love *her.* There were a lot of shows that stayed on that were not good at all, but the people were so attractive, warm, lovely characters, that the show stayed on even if they were bad. When you get the combination of good script and lovely, warm people, you get something extraordinary. You get something that is a big success.

But to answer that question, situation comedy has to have warm people. To get real laughs; the audience has to identify with the hero. Like his targets, accept his targets. I directed a very black comedy called *Where's Poppa?* and the target was motherhood. But they liked the hero enough to laugh with him. In fact, he was trapped. That was warm and zany, too, even though I didn't write it.

In the first Dick Van Dyke series, you used the committee approach to writing the final scripts. The writers as well as the producer and performers sat in. Why did you use this collaboration format? And was that something you learned with Sid Caesar?

Oh, yes. But the idea for that was set by the three-camera technique. Danny Thomas had that. It's like a play. In a play you must bring in your characters, your actors, at one point and have them become a creative part. They have to try the words on for size, when you're sitting around a table reading. I did that with this last picture I did. If you've got intelligent actors who have thoughts—they're only to be selected, to be used or not used depending on what you feel as the director. But you try to get the best out of people. From anyone. I would take suggestions from the janitor. Sometimes a prop man came up with an idea that was hilarious and we used it. I don't care who gives me the idea. In the end it's the selectivity of the director. He has to make the final choice.

Why don't more shows do that?

A lot of shows are now using the three-camera technique because it is a good one. Mary Tyler Moore, "All in the Family" are using it. It depends on how secure the producer or the writer is—to be able to take suggestions without feeling that he's being attacked.

You've been a producer, director, writer, as well as a performer. In a comedy show can the performer judge a piece of material better than the people who created it for him?

No, but they can tell you whether they're comfortable with it yet, whether they can do something with it. Dick Van Dyke is the best judge of whether he's comfortable with something, but he's not always correct about the whole thing. He might think that particular show is not working because the audience isn't there yet, but he'll stay with it until the end. The actor knows pretty well when he's comfortable. That's what he knows.

With the three-camera technique you do the show straight through, don't you?

Uh huh.

What if the audience doesn't react on lines. Do you dub in the laughs?

That happens . . . No, we just—

Reshoot it?

No. If it's funny and the audience doesn't laugh, that doesn't mean it's not funny at home sometimes. We'll leave it alone. We'll let a joke die sometimes. Most of the time our shows are too long, and if jokes really die because they're questionable or not too funny, we cut them out. We just zip them out. We show twenty-four minutes of film. We shoot twenty-eight minutes—so four minutes disappear.

Many times the audience doesn't get a joke because of the placement of the camera. The players are obscured for a minute. Sometimes it's the sound. Someone coughs on a punch line. But when you see it at home on the set, if it's funny, you might laugh without hearing the audience laughing.

Suppose someone felt he could write funny and wanted to earn his living as a comedy writer. How would he go about it?

By writing funny. It's as simple as that. You don't need any entree when you're a writer. All you need is a pencil and paper or typewriter and a piece of paper. Write it and send it to somebody. If you're a good writer, somebody—

Would he begin by writing jokes?

It depends upon where he's going. A humorous kid . . . It's an evolution. You start with a grimace. You make people laugh by an angularity of your body. You make a face when you're very young and then you want to make people laugh so you tell them a joke or two. It's usually a one-line joke or two. Then you start telling a story; then you go into sketch form; then you go into the half-hour comedy form—situation comedy. The best situation comedy is really a one-act play investigation of characters and doesn't really have to have a punch. Most of the comedy series will try to have a punch line at the end of each show. But the most successful ones are the ones that really go deeply into the characters. You asked a different question.

About the young writer.

I think the size of your work grows with your age. There are very few prodigy comedy talents. To be able to make fun of something, you have to be able to understand it, and understanding comes with age. It's very rare to read about a prodigy comedian. I've known two or three in my life who at seventeen or sixteen had the ability to make you laugh. Larry Gelbart, the writer, was one of them. This new comedian, Albert Brooks, I've known since he was twelve or thirteen. He was able to make us laugh since he was a kid. Most kids can't.

You need certain references. To comment on certain things you have to know about the things you're commenting on. Television has given them a great latitude. Kids watch television and they get an awful lot of things to satirize—commercials, politics, situation comedy. As they get older, they realize which ones are the good ones, and through selectivity they make fun of the funny ones. My kid, Rob, has the same background as Albert. They both were television bred.

Young writers are very often asked to write scripts or special material without compensation. Is this speculation a pitfall newcomers should avoid?

If a writer's young, he's gotta speculate. He should want to speculate. Nobody should demand anybody to speculate. I don't. But if you are a writer, nobody has to ask you to write. The reason a person is called a writer is because he has a great desire to write. Writers express themselves. They contact the world by putting pen to paper. That *urge* makes them writers.

Asking new writers to speculate is neither here nor there. It has nothing to do with writing. It has to do with economics. You're talking about the commercial aspects. You got something to say and somebody says, "I'm not going to pay you." You'd write it whether they paid you or not—if you're really a writer. The real writer is the fellow who has novels in his attic that haven't been published. That's a real writer. Whether he's good or not is something else. But usually he has to express himself through writing because he can't contact the world easily on a social basis.

At schools and colleges, students can take courses in playwriting, how to write short stories or novels. Is comedy writing a subject that can be taught?

No, I don't think it can be taught. But giving somebody the platform to do it is a good thing. If you're at school and somebody says write a joke, write something, you're forced to write, and it might be a good thing. I don't think you can *teach* comedy writing. I don't think you can teach any kind of writing, really. The great writers have never been taught to write.

But there are certain techniques, formulas. For example, if you write a one-line joke, you try to save your key word for the last word.

Yeah, but the good writers know instinctively. They talk that way. They just do that. But I tell you, the real great comedy writers and great comedians break that rule all the time. I remember Herb Shriner used to tell the same joke three different ways to keep it fresh. He'd change the punch line and put it in a different place. It's a good thing to remember. If you know the joke is going to be a certain rhythm—da ta da ta da bop, da ta da ta da bop—people are going to laugh just by rote. But they're not going to enjoy. They're going to laugh because they're programmed to laugh.

But if you put that joke in a place they don't expect it, like Woody Allen does very often—his jokes are not always in the spot you expect them. They're in the middle of the sentence sometimes. In the middle of a thought. He's doing a straight line, and the joke will be in the straight line. That's again the surprise element.

Teaching people what the cliché is is very good. "This is the cliché—you put the straight line here and the joke comes out here and you use the letter k if you have a hard word. If you have a hard word it's going to be funnier than if you say—"

Now you're stating some rules.

Yes. I know all the rules, but I don't know I know them. I know them because maybe I've discussed them with the guys. It's good to be aware of the rules so you can break them. If you don't break the rules you're not going to get very far.

There must be other rules that we could discuss.

I can only talk about the shows I write. I use mystery, surprise, saying the thing that's unexpected or the most expected, either one.

They're complete opposites.

Yeah, either one. When they expect the unexpected, give them the most expected. It's a joke.

Could you clarify that?

A non-joke could be a joke sometime. You say, "I just flew in from Washington, D.C. You know what Washington, D.C. is? It's the capital of the United States." That's a non-joke. But there's something humorous about it, because everybody, at that moment, expected some kind of a Bob Hope punch line to make it a joke.

Because it had the set-up and the rhythm.

Yeah, the rhythm.

So you get fooled by it.

Yeah, you're tuned in, you're so programmed to know a joke is coming there, and when the joke doesn't come—that's a joke. Knowing the clichés is what I'm saying. If you know the clichés, you know how to sidestep them and use them. I've done it a lot on the Dick Van Dyke shows. It looks like I'm going into a very cliché ending, and they get lulled. They say, "Look where he's going." And then you don't go there. Sometimes when they know you never got to the cliché ending, you go to the cliché ending and it is a surprise.

How do you learn clichés?

By living and observing. A comedy writer or any writer must be an observer, and he can't be *taught* to be an observer. You are an observer at birth.

What do you mean by an "observer"?

One who recognizes everything around him. He notices the size of things, sees the shape of things, the smell of things. How people react, why they react. The different things that exist in the world. I don't think you can *train* for that. You *are* that. Certain people are busybodies and certain people are not. Some people want to know everything.

You believe someone is actually born with that ability?

Absolutely. Born or it's honed into them at a very early age. Or happens to them environmentally. Perhaps being in a household of nuts, where everybody's got some kind of neurosis that makes you look about you. There are many reasons for talent to flourish. But talent has to be there to begin with.

This book is being created to help people—

The people who need help are not going to get it from your book. Let me put it a different way. If it helps people to get *out* of the business who think they should be in the business, that's a help, too. To stop, to abort people from going into something they don't know. It might get some people to realize they're not cut out to be comedy writers and they'll go do something else. I consider myself a hack. It's a good way to make a living. You can learn certain techniques to write comedy. There are a lot of guys doing that and making a *fair* living at it.

I think writing is one of the things where nobody has to help you. You can't say, "I didn't make it because I didn't have pull." You might be able to say that if you're an actor. You may be a very good actor, but unless you can talk somebody into putting you on the stage or letting you do a part that they've written, you don't have a chance. Some actors don't know how to sell themselves. A writer has nobody to blame but himself. He puts it on the paper, and if it's funny somebody will laugh.

In show business, most performers become successful by relentless drive and dedication. Do comedy

writers also succeed by constantly selling themselves?

No; comedy writers succeed by writing funny
material. There are some comedy writers who are
talking writers and don't know how to write. But
they're good for comedians because they can sometimes put words into comedians' mouths. They're
jesters. They're just not writers. They're writers
without using a pencil.

Neil
SIMON

M arvin Neil ("Doc") Simon was born July 4, 1927, in the Bronx. The son of a garment sales-man, Simon was brought up in Washington Heights and graduated from DeWitt Clinton High School.

At fifteen, while still in high school, he began writing in collaboration with his older brother, Danny. After serving in and being discharged from the army, Simon worked in the mail room of Warner Brothers, where Danny was active in the publicity department. The Simon brothers, while employed by Warner Brothers, spent their evenings writing comedy material and finally secured their first professional employment at CBS in the company's comedy writer development program.

They wrote an early Phil Silvers series and spent the next few years writing summer revues at Tamiment, "Your Show of Shows," starring Sid Caesar and Imogene Coca, and sketches for the Broadway revue *Catch a Star*.

The collaborators then parted. Danny took off for Hollywood, and Neil remained in New York to write "Caesar's Hour," some forty "Sergeant Bilko" episodes, and, after that script, eighteen months of Garry Moore shows.

From that point Neil Simon began writing plays. As a result, drama history may record him as the most prolific and successful playwright since William Shakespeare. Following is Neil Simon's incredible list of credits:

Plays:
  Come Blow Your Horn (also a motion picture)
  Barefoot in the Park (also a motion picture)
  The Odd Couple (also a motion picture)
  The Star Spangled Girl
  Plaza Suite (also a motion picture)
  The Last of the Red Hot Lovers (also a motion picture)
  The Gingerbread Lady
  The Prisoner of Second Avenue (also a motion picture)
  The Sunshine Boys (also a motion picture)
  The Good Doctor
  God's Favorite
Musicals:
  Little Me
  Promises, Promises
  Sweet Charity
Motion Pictures:
  After the Fox
  The Out of Towners
  The Heartbreak Kid

This talk was conducted near the fireplace in the sitting room of Neil Simon's East Sixties town-house in New York City. Simon wore a hunter green mock turtleneck sweater, cinnamon-and-black checked trousers, and brown loafers. It is surprising to see Simon still wearing simple attire, since *Variety* estimates that he earns $3.9 to $4.5 million a year.

He is soft-spoken and sincere and smiles often while expressing opinions emphatically. His quiet manner suggests true modesty, and in just a few moments you know that Neil Simon, the real man, is basically unaffected by his enormous success.

You started by writing jokes for comedians and then sketches for revues and television. In what way do you feel this background helped prepare you for playwriting?

Well, just the experience of writing, just sitting down and trying to write was the first step. There's a vast difference between the writing I originally did and playwriting. Writing gags is a purely mechanical thing, it seems to me. Playwriting is writing about characters. It's hard to say what value it had for me except I guess the experience of getting my work in front of an audience and trying out jokes. It was someplace to start.

When you first started you worked for Goodman Ace.

Yeah. I was nineteen years old.

What influence did Goody have on your development?

Very little. I spent seventeen weeks with Goody. I wouldn't say anyone was more responsible than anyone else for the development. I've been in contact with so many people over the years that everybody has been influential. If anyone was an inspiration to me, I would say it was Kaufman and Hart. I never met either one, but reading their plays and saying, "That's what I want for myself one day." I tried to emulate their style of playwriting. In the beginning years, working for television, you have no style. The only style you have is that of whomever you are working for. If I worked for Sid Caesar, that was my style. If I worked for Phil Silvers, that was my style.

You had to adapt the material to their characters.

You had to forget yourself. They employed you to work for them. You could not differentiate any other writer's material from your own when you worked for Sid Caesar. I used to sit home and watch the shows at night, after seven of us had worked on it during the day, and forget what was my contribution. When I began writing plays and started with *Come Blow Your Horn,* I forgot all about that and started off like it was the first day of writing for me. I said, "Now I start using *myself,* my own personalities, my own attitudes, my own philosophies in life."

You spent two years with Phil Silvers on the "Sergeant Bilko" TV series. Did that assignment help develop your technique?

It was a very valuable experience, because it was the first time that I worked on something *longer* than just sketches. Previous to that I had worked mostly on the Sid Caesar show and shows like that, where you wrote ten- or twelve-minute sketches and monologues. I also did sketches without any character, just a funny situation.

On the Bilko show the situation came out of Phil Silvers's character. Paul Ford played a very definite character. So you were sort of locked into people, and that was good training in how to write for characters, sort of short movies based on character.

About a year after that I went to work for Max Liebman. He did two years of specials. We adapted former Broadway musicals for television. We did

Best Foot Forward, Dearest Enemy, Connecticut Yankee—all the shows that once were big hits on Broadway—changed them, updated them for TV. Even operettas, classics like *Naughty Marietta.* Some of them were terrible, some pretty good, but it was a new experience for me, new training, all very helpful.

As a result of all this experience could you describe some specific points of comedy construction you developed?

I'm never very conscious of comedy technique, devices, gimmicks. It's there, but I think most of it is instinctive. I never sit to figure it out. There are certain rules that I have. Sometimes I don't know the rule when I'm writing, but when I go back and look at it and say, "This is not working," then I may examine the rule. This does not apply to everything, but it's getting either people, forces of opposite desires and opposite personalities, opposite characters, and putting them in contact with each other—in contrast with each other—and letting the sparks fly in what I like to consider an intolerable situation.

A good joke always has an easy flow, and there is a cadence or a rhythm in the language. Does the same rule hold true for dialogue in a comedy play?

Yes, of course. Comedy dialogue in a play has to seem as though it was not written. Whereas a Bob Hope joke—you're kind of aware of it, and you know he just doesn't stand up there and say all these things. You sort of see the writer behind it all. When you are writing a play of character it must seem to the audience that the character is making this up, that the writer is completely unseen.

The minute you do sort of see the *sweat on the word,* you are aware of it being a joke. There was only one real joke joke in *The Odd Couple,* and it was pointed out to me in the review of Howard Taubman, who was then the critic for the *New York Times*.

That joke didn't have to be worded that way, but it was one of the very few lines you can take out of context of the play and tell to someone. The line was "He's so nervous that he wears a seat belt in a drive-in movie." It holds up as a joke, but almost every other line in the play you cannot say out of context and think it is very funny on its own.

You did the screenplay for *Barefoot in the Park* as well as for *The Odd Couple*. Were there any specific problems you had to overcome in adapting them from stage versions?

There were problems, and some I didn't overcome. It's very tricky when you are changing a stage play into a motion picture. Your instinct is to say, "I don't want to make this look like a stage play, so let's get it out of the room as much as possible and get outside." But sometimes that backfires on you. It did, to my way of thinking, in *Barefoot in the Park,* where we actually showed a scene where Paul, the lead boy character, was drunk and went walking barefoot in the park. It seemed ludicrous when it happened, to me anyway. On the stage it didn't, because you didn't actually see Paul come in barefoot. He had his shoes on and he took them off later, and then you saw he was not wearing any socks.

And it was all in the audience's mind.

And so much better. On the other hand, the exact opposite: I took a scene in *The Odd Couple* that took place in the first act where Felix, the Jack Lemmon-Art Carney character, was suddenly having a terrible case of his eustachian tubes closing up, and he was trying to clear his nasal passages. He was doing this *in the play* in the room with Oscar, the

Walter Matthau character, because we couldn't go
out of the room. In the film I had that scene take
place in a luncheonette where he was carrying on
and making these wild noises. This involved other
people in the luncheonette with a guy turning
around to watch—which embarrassed Oscar. That
played much funnier. It's a matter of choice. Sometimes changes work; sometimes they don't.

**What are the advantages of writing the screen adap-
tation of your own play rather than turning it over to
another writer?**

There's one very big advantage. Having seen so
many productions of the play in front of so many
audiences, I know almost everything that works in
the play. When you do it for the screen, all the play's
high and low points and weaknesses—they have to
be trimmed; they have to be changed. For example,
in *Barefoot in the Park* we were trimming it down
and Hal Wallis, the producer, mentioned that a
certain line didn't seem funny to him. I said, "That
line works; I promise you!" So he left it in, and it got
one of the biggest laughs in the movie. So that's one
advantage.

**In a *Newsday* story you were quoted as saying,
"Writing for the theater is much more satisfying
than movie script writing." Would you explain that?**

You have a much better chance to control the
material when you're working on stage. I can see
exactly what the audience is going to see in my
mind's eye. I know it's usually a proscenium theater
and that the audience is seeing all this at the same
time. In writing for the screen I have to try to
visualize it through the *director's* eye. When you
have three people on stage talking at the same time,
the audience sees three people. In the film the cam-

era may be on one of the persons, the one who is speaking, or it may be on somebody else, or maybe on one who is not speaking. Very important points may be lost all along the way.

Another thing that is terribly important. I have four weeks of rehearsal with the play and approximately four weeks out of town in front of audiences every night. I consider a film equivalent to the first week's rehearsal of a play. You don't get to rehearse a film. The film I did with Jack Lemmon and Sandy Dennis was an outdoor film. It took place all over New York City. We could not rehearse it. We only read it over about three times. We couldn't go on Forty-eighth Street and Third Avenue and have them running down the streets—

And there is no sure way to find out where the laughs are.

Yeah. So we just had to shoot it after three or four days of work. I wouldn't dream of opening a play after one week's rehearsal, even if the actors all knew their lines. It needs much more time. I need those four weeks of audience reaction so I can cut and trim.

Does that mean it's easier to write a screenplay than a stage play?

No; neither one is easy. They're both hard, but there are more benefits to writing for the stage, at least for me. But apparently not for everyone. Most of the writers involved in comedy writing that I know do not write for the theater; they write for the screen—I think because the element of financial chance is taken out for them. You could work for a year on a play and get nothing from it in return, if the play flops. Writing for a film, you are guaranteed something whether the picture works or not.

How much different is the original script bought by the producer from the polished play that opens on Broadway?

It depends on the play, and it depends on your growth as a writer and your craftsmanship. *Come Blow Your Horn*—the first play—without exaggeration, had twenty different versions. It also had about twenty different producers. The first man who ever saw the play was Herman Shumlin. It had a different title, and it had not one word remaining in the original script that was in the final version of the play.

On the other hand, *Plaza Suite*—I did two versions of it, one in complete rewrite and then some work out of town on it. *Barefoot in the Park*—I changed about forty percent. *The Odd Couple*—the first and second acts were virtually the same from what we went into rehearsal with. The third act I threw out completely in rehearsal and did three new third acts. *Plaza Suite* had the least amount of rewrite.

Barefoot in the Park and Come Blow Your Horn tried out in the Bucks County Playhouse prior to the customary New Haven, Boston, Philadelphia, then Broadway route. What advantage is there to testing a comedy in an off-the-beaten track summer theater?

It just gives you extra time in front of an audience. I still had my four weeks in New Haven and Boston with *Barefoot in the Park,* but I also had two extra weeks of rehearsal and two extra weeks of playing it in front of an audience.

What percentage of the total finished product is contributed by the director?

It depends on the director. You couldn't put a

percentage on it. I've been very lucky with the directors I've worked with. Mike Nichols's contribution has not been just in the directing of the play, in saying to the actors, we should interpret this way or that, but he would get with me and say, "I think the second act falls down at this particular spot, and I feel the leading character does not accomplish. . ." et cetera.

There are no actual words in the play contributed by Mike, but at least he starts the wheel spinning, and I say, "Oh, if you feel this doesn't work, I have to go back and rewrite." So I rewrite it. Every word in the play is mine, and yet rewrites have been inspired and helped enormously by people like Mike, like Robert Morra. We go over the script dozens of times.

While the play is in tryouts, do the actors contribute pieces of business or lines that help make the production more effective?

Lines, almost never. I've rarely come across an actor contributing a line. I would say half of one percent of any of the lines in a play have been contributed by an actor. Business, yes. Interpretation, yes. And lines being *cut* are very often a contribution of an actor.

Before you start the actual writing of a play, how detailed a framework have you planned?

Well, it's changed over the years. In *Come Blow Your Horn* I did a *complete* outline, because I had never written a play before and I wanted to learn about playwriting. I never intended it to be a play to be put on anywhere. I did it as an experiment to see if I could write a play. I wrote a complete, detailed outline and found I couldn't stick to it because the play wanted to go off in its own direction. I spent so much time in rewriting, trying to keep to this plan, that I decided I would use less and less of a detailed outline.

In *Barefoot in the Park* I used about half of the detailed outline and found again the play wanted to go off on its own. Then I found as the plays were progressing I was writing less and less story lines and fewer plot lines and going more and more for character. When you are going for character, there is very little you can outline.

In *Plaza Suite* there was no outline at all. I just put the paper in the typewriter and started going. I'm two-thirds through with a new play; I have one more act. There was no outline at all. I just made a couple of notes about some of the character's background.

Drama critic Whitney Bolton once wrote an article on your writing technique in which he pointed out that your "comedy came from character, rather than character rising from comedy." Is this an accurate estimate of your approach?

Yes. I don't think in terms of comedy as I'm working, not anymore, anyway. I think of it as a serious play but not told in serious terms—and that I can't explain. *The Odd Couple* is *not really* a comedy; it's a serious play but told in comedic terms.

In that same article Bolton said, "Teachers of playwriting say that there must be a plot and all of it must be motivated and come together like a jigsaw puzzle." But Bolton felt that by "ignoring this jigsaw puzzle approach, you created an even better play." Do you agree that your plays aren't tightly plotted?

I wrote one that was tightly plotted—*Come Blow Your Horn*. But it bored me to write tightly plotted plays, and I think it's very old-fashioned now. You

see very, very few tightly plotted plays, if there is
any plot at all. Plays are going much, much more
towards character, and that is the only thing that
really interests me.

**In *Plaza Suite* the two main characters of each play
were in direct opposition to each other. Is this conflict of characters your secret to creating a comedy
situation?**

No, it's *life's* secret. There is no interest without
conflict in almost any form of life. Take sports: two
teams are in conflict. Take a love affair: the man and
woman are in conflict. If they are both saying "yes,"
right away there is no interest. They go upstairs and
that's their business. The animal looking for food:
there is conflict—he has to find it. This has to be put
on the stage in order to create any kind of interest.

**What is the difference in the dialogue of two people
in a one-act comedy play as compared to a sketch
done by say, the vaudeville comedians Smith and
Dale?**

Well, Smith and Dale's comedy does not ema-
nate from character at all. It is whatever joke helps fit
the situation. They just throw it in, and they take
things that have nothing to do with what they are
doing and they'll use it. They just happen to use very
funny jokes.

**In building a routine, comedians try to get a laugh
and then top it with another laugh and then try to top
it again. Is that a technique you use in building the
laugh sequences in your plays?**

Yes. I'm not very conscious of doing it, but it
does happen because sometimes the situations are
so fraught with humor. For example, one of the
things most talked about in *The Odd Couple* was the
opening poker game scene. A number of critics said,

"How brave he was to start off with a hilarious scene and then try to top it with a play that followed."

Had I known that that scene would be *that* hilarious, *I* might have been frightened of it. I didn't write it thinking it was going to be hilarious. I said, "This is the best possible way, the most interesting way that I can do the exposition of the play, to show the leading character, Oscar, as a complete slob."

I picked the poker game with the men complaining about the house, that the place was filthy, it stunk, the milk was in the refrigerator for weeks. Then they started talking about Felix. They wondered where he was . . . setting up their nervousness about Felix committing suicide and talking about what kind of character he was. And so I used it as a device for exposition, but it came out very, very funny. Much funnier than we ever thought.

There were times Mike Nichols and I didn't think it was very funny. We were considering cutting it during rehearsal, and then we started to like it again and we left it in. We were shocked when the audience responded the way they did.

Why is it you write a line or sequence and think it's funny and it doesn't work, and other times you're not sure and it gets a laugh?

Yeah. Well, I would say I'm right about sixty percent of the time, but I'm never quite sure of the *volume* of laughs. There have been things I felt pretty safe about. For example, in *Promises, Promises,* the scene with Marian Mercer, the girl at the bar in the beginning of the second act—one of the highlights of the play. It seems now that it was one of the toughest spots in the play for me to do.

I did it over and over and I couldn't find anything. Finally, when I found this girl Marian Mercer in rehearsal, I was able to go back and write the scene, and it worked in almost every spot we hoped it would work.

You wrote the books for *Sweet Charity* **and** *Little Me.* **What is the difference between creating comedy dialogue for a musical and a comedy play?**

I used to think there was a difference, and then I found out in *Promises, Promises* that there shouldn't be as great a difference. After *Little Me* and *Sweet Charity,* my feeling about musicals was that people did not speak like they do in real life, the way they do in plays—that they could not be as leisurely in the dialogue, that they spoke shorter sentences and they spoke louder.

These were my visual and oral impressions of what it was like in a musical, and that's pretty much what *Little Me* was. *Little Me* was a satire, and so it was highly stylized anyway, but *Sweet Charity,* if you take out the songs, I would never consider doing as a play. The characters didn't speak like people did, but it did fit the style of the show. It also was not very gratifying to me as a writer. I would much rather write plays and write about real people. The people in *Sweet Charity* were not real. It was really a dance show told in terms of the story.

So I was pretty much off doing musicals until I spoke with David Merrick and we kicked around some ideas. I said, "I only want to do a musical that would work as a play and then embellish it with songs and then it would work, for me at least."

Then we thought of *The Apartment.* I said, "I want to write that as I would a play, and so I think it could work even in those terms." And Clive Barnes sort of pointed that out. If you took the songs out of the show, it would still hold up as a play, because the people talk as real characters would. I think they are enhanced by the songs. Emotional moments are much better sung on the stage than just spoken.

You said you did a dozen versions of the third act of *The Odd Couple.* **Was that a particularly difficult problem to solve, or is this intensive rewriting standard with you?**

Well, it's standard, but that was a specific problem. I do it anyway. I did *Promises* one summer. I just kept working over and over on it, and then you get out of town; you keep trying things and doing new things—so I'm constantly rewriting.

But usually I'm rewriting the existing material, polishing it. I'm going over each line, each sound, each word. That was not the case of the third act of *The Odd Couple.* The story points just did not work. I had various twists and turns that seemed to just stand there on the stage without working at all.

Did you find those things didn't work as a result of having tried them out on stage?

Oh, yeah. The first time we found out that the third act didn't work was just sitting around and reading it. The very first day of reading *The Odd Couple* the first act sounded fine. The second act sounded even better, and the third act souned *terrible.*

There had to be some truth in it, because the first and second acts couldn't have sounded so good and the third act sound so bad without any real reason for it. So Mike Nichols went ahead and rehearsed the first and second acts while I went home and did a third act.

I brought another version in that didn't sound much better, but we were stuck, and we had to go out of town with a third act we knew would not work. But we had to open with a play, and we hoped that an audience would tell us something.

On the train down to Wilmington, where we were trying out the play, Mike and I kept kicking around ideas and finally came up with something, and I said, "This sounds right. I want to write." I worked two or three days before we opened, and I finished the third act.

Mike said, "We are going to open with this." The actors threw up their arms and said, "It's impossible. We'll never learn it."

Mike said, "I'd rather you go out and do a good third act badly than do a bad third act well. We know eventually we're going to do this new third act."

They learned it and we did it and a great deal of it worked, but we were still a long way from where we should be. When we got to Boston, I wrote still another scene and we rehearsed it, and everyone was hysterical during the rehearsal. The actors were falling down, and Mike said it was just too funny.

It was great, and we did it that night on stage and it died completely, did not work, and it threw us into desperation. We said, "If what we think is funny is not going to work, where do we turn?" So I took a couple of days off from the show, went back to New York to get it out of my mind. I went back, and then we went on to Washington. I kept on working, and finally it seemed to work out.

Then what people often describe as *genius* **is in reality plain** *hard work?*

Of course. That's all it ever is—hard work. The inspiration, if any, comes at the beginning. Putting it all down and seeing the whole thing. Making it work and making it right then becomes just hard work.

You have been quoted as saying you "always feel you are facing imminent disaster whn you are working on a show, you assume things are wrong and need fixing." Does this attitude come from sad experience, or is worrying a natural characteristic of someone who creates laughter?

With me it's a natural characteristic, but it's based on a good philosophy: Leave the good things alone in the show—they'll take care of themselves—and only work on the things that are not working. I can't be complacent. There are so many people who say, "We're doing fine; let's leave it alone. Don't play with that!" You're out of town to work and to make it better. I always assume that things are not going to go for the best, and by doing that you work on it instead of hanging around and going to a movie.

Do you think the people "out of town" are aware that they are, in essence, "guinea pigs" for a project being produced for profit and that will eventually appear on Broadway hundreds of miles from them?

Oh, yeah. I get many more comments from people out of town about what to do with the show than in New York. In New York they say, "It's a *fait accompli.*" They say the show is good or it's bad. Out of town they say this could be good or this could be terrible. They're always saying, "Do you mind if I give you a suggestion?" Which you *do* mind.

To me the most important times are not that first night in New York and not necessarily that first night in Boston or New Haven. It's the first time the very few people I respect read the play. If I get past them, which is in a way its own opening night . . . then it gets to the actors; it gets the first day of sitting around the table and reading the material. When you do that you're hearing it now for the first time and that again is another opening night.

As I said before with *The Odd Couple,* it all sounded so wonderful. I'll give you an example: Two nights before *The Odd Couple* went into rehearsal, I was with Mike Nichols at a party and I said, "Well, in two days we go."

Mike said, "Yeah, it's exciting!

I said, "Is there anything in it that you want me to change, that you don't like and you think is not going to work?"

He said, "No. Why? Is there something that you're nervous about?"

I said, "No; I like it all."

He said, "So do I."

I said, "Then how come both of us, fairly successful professionals, know that on the morning of the reading we're going to find all sorts of things wrong with the play and we don't know it now?" And it's the truth.

What is the answer to that?

The answer is, you have to be aware and not lie to yourself when you're faced with the truth that some things are not going to work. You can't say, "Let's hope that we'll get away with it, that we'll get a hot audience that night and get good reviews." You have to work on it. The next biggest frightening time is when you get in front of the first live audience. Whether it is an invited group of professionals in New York before you go out of town or your first preview out of town. They will tell you very accurately what you have, and after that it is just a matter of degree—whether you can fix it enough if it needs that much fixing. But that pretty much will be the truth that night.

You have become the most successful comedy playwright of modern times, both critically and

financially. Has this acceptance made your work any easier?

I don't know, because I have the same rules and the same standards that I've always had. To make it as good as possible in the given amount of time I have to work on it. I don't say, "Maybe I'll get away with this one. They *owe* me one." I never have that feeling. I've got to work as hard as I ever did and still try to please myself very much and that small group of people I trust.

Newspaper columnist Gerald Nachman quoted you as saying, "I'm successful and still don't know what's funny. The only time I'm secure is when I sit down at the typewriter." Now comedians are also notorious for being insecure. Is the comedy field so exacting and so exasperating that it turns seemingly normal human beings into nervous, neurotic nail-biters?

Yeah; but I don't think comedy writers are really normal, everyday human beings. Most of them that I know are highly neurotic in one form or another. I don't mean they are outwardly neurotic, but I think there are certain tensions and drives that make them what they are. They all have hang-ups.

Is that part of the make-up of a comedy writer?

The ones I've seen, yeah. It's very true about comics, too. Even more so with comedians. They not only have the urge to be funny and to be accepted, but it has to be *in person*. It has to be in front of an audience. I get enough kicks in back of the theater hearing an audience laugh. I don't have to be up there on the stage and take a bow. It's enough for me to know that what I have done and what I feel are being accepted by an audience. That's enormously gratifying.

What motivates someone like you to be satisfied to hear audience laughter from the back of the theater as opposed to someone who has to get up and get laughs in front of the audience?

Well, I'm not quite sure what his drive is. There are comedians who are not funny at all but who say very funny things written by other people. They go out and say those same things over and over again. I can't imagine what kind of joy they get, except if they do it in terms of an actor. I don't think they do, because an actor usually puts himself *behind* the mask of a character he's playing. He is projecting a little of himself in this other character. The comic doing the same jokes over and over—I don't know what kind of satisfaction he gets except for making a living.

If I'm at a party and on a rare occasion I say something funny and there's a big laugh and people say, "You've got to tell so and so over there," I can't do it for the life of me—say it again. I've just done it. The moment is gone for me. Let me give you an example:

I was on the Johnny Carson show, and he asked me about the first joke I had ever written on the Sid Caesar show. I related the joke and it got an enormous laugh. The laugh I got from the audience was not as satisfying to me as two moments. One, when I made up the joke years before, and the first time the audience laughed at it on the air when Sid Caesar did it. When I did it I was just repeating something. I could have repeated somebody else's joke and got the same laugh from the audience. That's not my particular way of getting gratification.

When it comes to studying writing, you once said, "All courses do is teach you how to write plays like

everyone else writes." Do you feel then for someone wanting to be a playwright it would be a waste of time to study?

I don't think it is a waste of time to study. The only important thing for a playwright and for any writer is to write. The benefit of a playwriting course is that he will get his things aired in front of an audience or read by a teacher with some experience. But anyone trying to teach you *how* to write a play will only turn you out in the mold of other playwrights. I've never read books on playwriting. They never interested me. You only learn how to do it the way they did it instead of the way you want to do it.

In *Come Blow Your Horn* you said that the "characters of Mama and Papa Baker were based on your mother and father, as well as some aunts and uncles." Is this the classic example of the playwright writing about what he knows best?

Well, as I said, this was my first play attempt— as an experiment. I said to myself, "I've got to start from a point of my own experience." I was trying to break away from writing like Sid Caesar, Red Buttons, Phil Silvers—whoever I worked for—and start writing about myself. So I specifically wrote about my own background.

The mother and father in the play were very much like my own mother and father but were also composites of my aunts and uncles and of every other Jewish middle-class New York mother and father that I ever met. I found out, much to my amusement and gratification, that they seem to typify parents everywhere, because the play was a big hit in Australia and Europe.

In a *New York Times* article by Lewis Funke you

said, *"The Star Spangled Girl* **was written from an emotional identity rather than a personal identity."** **Would you explain the difference?**

The Star Spangled Girl was the only play I sat down to write before I really had an idea for a play. I said to myself, "What would be a good idea for a play?" I never did that before. Ideas for plays have always just presented themselves to me by observing things in my own life and the lives of the people around me. *Come Blow Your Horn, Barefoot in the Park*—my own experiences. *The Odd Couple* were two people I knew.

Do you think a good deal of the success of *Come Blow Your Horn* **was due to the fact that so many people were able to identify with the characters?**

Of course, of course. I wish I was able to write the play today with the experience I've had. But the people did have some flesh and blood in them and on them. *Star Spangled Girl* was an intellectual exercise for me. I said, "What would happen if a left-wing, liberal young college student met a right-wing, very attractive girl, and they became physically attracted to each other?" The idea is still not a bad one, but I chose the wrong girl. She just did not exist. I never met that girl, and so I was never able to capture the sound of her, to make her real flesh and blood.

Then that is the difference in "emotional" identity and "personal" identity.

Yes, yes. I vowed after that I would never again write a play, excluding a musical because that has its own problems, but never write a play I did not have some personal identification with, that I must have seen, known, come in contact with in some way the people I'm writing about. That girl was purely a figment of my imagination.

Most of the critics agree that the laughs in your plays come out of the situation rather than the actual jokes. Is it easier to extract laughter from a situation than with random jokes?

It's almost impossible. If you asked me now to make up a joke, I couldn't do it. It's not just the situation; it has to be the character in the situation. But again, I don't think of them in terms of jokes.

For example, this is certainly not a joke: In *The Odd Couple*, Oscar (the sloppy one) decides to take Felix (the very clean one)—to oversimplify them— into his house as his roommate and live together because they are very, very good friends. After they are living together a few weeks, things begin to change. We established in the first act that the Friday night card games are a ritual of sloppiness but real fun. These fellows are very much at ease. Once Felix moves in and takes over, the place is as clean as can be. He puts two coats of Johnson's Glow Coat over everything.

At one point, when Felix goes into the other room, one of the fellows who is complaining says, "He washed the cards; he washed the cards!" That's not a joke, but it gets an enormous laugh.

Once when Felix goes out of the room, Oscar says to Murray the cop, "I'll give you two hundred dollars for your gun." He wants to kill him. That's not a funny joke. You're not going to laugh when I tell you that now, but it gets an enormous laugh in the theater because it emanates purely from the character in the situation.

Your brother Danny explains your success by saying, "People love the people in his plays. They are always done with love and sympathy. Doc never gets mad at anything." Isn't that approach to comedy diametrically opposite to the traditional

theory that the basis of comedy is *hostility* and *anger?*

It's hostility and anger, but you can still love the people if you sympathize and identify with them. It's very important that the audience *likes* the people up there. Villains seem to be a thing of the past. The world has become so muddy and confused it is hard to tell who the villains are.

When I was a kid, any foreign country opposing the American doctrine was the enemy. Germany was the enemy. In the Revolutionary days, England was the enemy. We're at war with countries; now we're the enemy. So I hate to put enemies on the stage. In this respect I was influenced by George Bernard Shaw, who never put enemies in his plays.

For example, Undershaft, the munitions maker in *Major Barbara:* his character points were so well given that you said, "He really believes in what he is saying, and he has certain points that help me understand him. I don't have to like him or sympathize with him, but I can understand him." I think *understanding* is the first step toward liking someone. But I don't necessarily go about trying to make the audience *like* the characters in my plays. But by presenting all the issues and their side of it, it somehow turns out that the audience does like the character.

Most successful comedians agree that the audience has to like you in order to laugh at you.

Yeah, but there are some exceptions. There are comics that I do not like and occasionally will laugh at because they will do things I admire technically and the moment is right, but in the long run I don't laugh at them. Whereas someone like Art Carney—I like him so much whatever he does I laugh at twice as much as if I didn't like him.

It appears that the serious playwright or author is looked upon with greater respect than his comedy counterpart. Why is that?

Possibly because we feel that laughter is a relief from the important things in life, so we tend to put down anything that has to do with laughter—except years later when you view it in perspective. I don't know how Chaplin was regarded when his two-reel comedies were being shown, if they said, this "profound genius" is making these comedies, as we say today. Aristophanes wrote comedies. We say he was a genius. I don't know what they thought of him then. It seems a comedy about politics is taken less lightly than a comedy about domestic matters.

What kind of daily writing discipline do you impose on yourself?

There used to be a routine when I had nothing else in life to do but just write. When I left television to become a playwright, I worked every single day. I worked on *Come Blow Your Horn* every day. I worked on *Barefoot in the Park* every day of the year practically, sometimes at night.

Did you get up at a certain time every morning?

Well, I did that because of the experience in television. I had to be at the office every day at ten o'clock, and I worked until five-thirty, six. I continued doing that as a playwright. Now there are so many other demands on my time I write in bulk. I write two, three months at a time; then I'm off in production on something or I'm traveling someplace.

In a typical day, how long can you stay at the typewriter?

It depends. Yesterday I worked seven hours. Another day, one hour, if I have an appointment in the afternoon. It also depends on how the work is

going. If I like what I'm doing, quite often I forget
about the time and just keep writing until the buzzer
buzzes and someone says, "Dinner is ready."
**Having achieved critical acclaim and financial suc-
cess, you still work as diligently as in the days when
recognition and money were eluding you. What is it
that motivates a man to continue creating even
though he apparently needs no ego assuaging or
monetary reward?**

I don't need the monetary reward, but I do need
the ego-building thing. That's the thing with all of
us. I'm not dead yet. I want to keep on doing things,
but I don't want to keep repeating them. It would not
be very satisfactory for me to keep writing plays
and for people to say, "Gee, that was marvelous,
another hit."

The ideal for me is for them to say, "This is your
best play." Then the next one should be my best play.
So I just keep on working and hoping that will
happen each time.

The
END

Anatomy of a Joke

Possibly the most complicated area of comedy writing to clarify is the complex technique of creating a joke. Technically, a joke consists of words that form sentences—sometimes an entire paragraph—and expresses a comedic thought that induces laughter. Since each writer goes about getting the end result in his own way, there is no set, incontrovertible explanation.

Unlike a scientific experiment in which each component can be listed, labeled, and categorized, inventing a joke is an intellectual exercise. And according to the inventors, it is exceedingly tough to verbalize.

Mort Lachman, head writer and producer of "The Bob Hope Show" for over twenty years, is quite candid in his attitude toward this inscrutable mystery. A short time after he joined Hope, Lachman approached Norman Sullivan, who had been with the comedian ten years before Mort arrived on the scene.

"Norman, I don't know what the hell I'm doing," wailed Lachman. "Every day I start out and try to write some jokes. And I don't know what a joke is. And I don't know how to write a joke. It's embarrassing. How do you do it?"

"Nobody knows that!" replied Sullivan, one of the most gifted of the jokesmiths. "If they did and it was teachable and learnable, they wouldn't hire us. They'd hire their sisters or cousins or uncles. What would they need us for? Total strangers. They need us because we're willing to sit like caged animals, thrashing about, learning by trial and error, working till all hours trying to find something that's funny. There are only a few nuts like us in the world."

Sullivan's opinion is shared by many members of the joke-writing fraternity. "It is not possible to teach someone the qualities that go into writing comedy," says Edwin Weinberger, producer of "The Mary Tyler Moore Show." "You can't teach intelligence, or imagination, or how to observe life from a funny point of view. You can't teach somebody to be an inspired, mad genius like Mel Brooks. But given some of these qualities, you can probably teach them something about the mechanics."

There are certain tangibles that do exist in coining gags. Successful scribes adhere to some basic rules that help make the task less tedious. Let us explore those areas.

The first thing a new writer has to learn is an economy of words," explains Mort Lachman. "Too many words convolute a thought. Every joke is different. You have one rhythm in one joke; you don't have it in the next one. As soon as you start to repeat your formulas then the elbows start to show, and then the jokes don't play anymore."

I asked Lachman, "Hope jokes are almost always based on current events. What is the purpose of that?"

"The only reason we use current events is because that's what people have in common, " he replied. "You can't make a joke about something people don't know. There are lots of jokes about Colonel Sanders because people know who you're talking about. It's common references that unite an audience. And that's what you have to find, that reference which unites an audience. You have to find those things that concern an audience, that embarrass them, things that an audience is upset about. Those are the things that work for comedy."

Some of the younger, highly proficient writers such as David Panich, Rudy DiLuca, Paul Pumpian, and others are daily practitioners of this point of view. "A timely *topical* reference can get you laughs where normally one doesn't exist," explains Arnie Kogen, who has written for many comedy stars, including Joey Bishop, Don Adams, Larry Storch, Jackie Vernon, Frank Gorshin, and Totie Fields. He is currently creating guffaws for "The Carol Burnett Show." "This is especially true of ludicrous TV commercials like Whip and Chill, the Tidy Bowl Man, the Heartbreak of Psoriasis, Can't Beat the Frizzies, Ann Blyth and her Hostess Ding-Dongs, Joe Namath selling pantyhose, and, of course,· a health nut walking through the forest eating twigs and branches instead of meat (excuse the expression, Euell).

"When these commercials are fresh and new," Kogen goes on, "you can often just *mention* them and get a laugh. Like, 'I'm sorry, I won't be in to work today. I'm in bed with the heartbreak of psoriasis.'

"Or at an awards show: 'For you winners tonight

there will be caviar and champagne. And for you losers, Euell Gibbons will pass among you with his wild hickory nuts.'

"The key, of course, is being inventive. Think of the commercial phrase or character and how it applies to our everyday life," says Kogen. "As an example: 'I just sent my wife on a seven-day cruise with the Tidy Bowl man.'

"'He's very unpopular. Even margarine won't talk to him.'

"'Euell Gibbons walked into the Beverly Hills Hotel and had a martini. He threw away the olive and ate the toothpick.'

"Besides commercials," says Kogen, a chief contributor to *Mad* magazine since 1959, "some very ripe areas for comedy are topical cultural happenings, fads, names in the news, et cetera. A congressman driving his car into a tidal basin with a stripper was good for chuckles in 1974 and 1975. Also, over the past few years we've had streaking, hotpants, Watergate, *The Godfather,* the meat shortage, vasectomies, and Marlon Brando giving his land away to the Indians. All are excellent topics for satire, sketches, and jokes.

"The important thing is to do them immediately. Make the jokes as fresh as possible. Some of the subjects I've mentioned may not be funny by the time someone gets around to reading this. That's why you have to keep up with the times. But don't listen to me. At this moment I'm wearing a Nehru jacket."

The words used in phrasing a joke are of the utmost importance. Just how important is made clear by Sherwood Schwartz, the creator-writer-producer of "The Brady Bunch." "Jokes should be written for reading aloud," says Schwartz. "Word or letter combinations difficult to pronounce should be avoided. The least contrived way, the most natural way, is the best way.

"The attention of the audience must remain sharply focused on one thought, and for this reason all confusing elements should be eliminated," states Schwartz, who also created and produced the long-running TV sitcom "Gilligan's Island."*

"For audience attention, the use of simple English is invariably best. Words people are familiar with don't worry them. If a strange word is used, it takes their minds away from the thought at hand, and they very often lose the thread they must follow in order to understand the joke. If the audience is comfortable with the language, their only concern is following the joke.

"Simple language does not mean ordinary or dull language," explains Schwartz, whose career began in 1939 writing for Bob Hope. "On the contrary, colorful words will often improve a joke. A joke about ice cream can often be improved by using the word *pistachio* or *tutti-frutti* instead of *vanilla*. Specific names instead of generalities are of good service. 'Evening in Paris' or 'Chanel No. 5' is better than just using a perfume.

"There are usually two key words or phrases in a joke. There is the key word in the straight lines, and there is a key word in the punch line. These two must be closely associated in the minds of the audience in order that they *get* the joke. Therefore, the

---

*Sherwood Schwartz shares a unique show business distinction with Elroy and Albert Schwartz. They are the only three comedy writing brothers in the industry

sentences should be phrased so that the key words are as close together as possible. There is one important limiting factor. That is, that the key word in the punch line must be placed as near the end of the line as can be managed. The reason for this is that the joke is usually over as soon as this word is spoken. If it were in the middle or beginning of the punch line, some of the audience would laugh too soon and the remainder of the sentence would be covered up. Example:

"He: *Why are you always raving about Burt Reynolds?*
"She: *Ah, when I kiss Burt, it's wonderful. That kiss has the kick of a mule in it.*
"He: *What about me?*
"She: *Well, that's like kissing a jackass, too!*

"Here the two key words are *mule* and *jackass*. It is the association of these two words which is the basis of the joke. *Mule* is the key word in the straight line. And *jackass* is next to the last word in the punch line."

The TV Comedy Series

Coming up with individual jokes for a stand-up comedian or a celebrity about to do an act in Las Vegas or a guest appearance on a TV variety show represents just one facet of the comedy writer's talent. What about the laughter kindled from the gags and humorous remarks that come from the mouths of Carroll O'Connor, Freddie Prinze, or Mary Tyler Moore?

These stars portray characters in hit television comedy series. And each episode must be meticulously conceived so that the funny lines come from these characters; more important, that the laughs are not *out of character*.

Stanley Ralph Ross, one of the most versatile of the television scripters, has written over 150 teleplays. "I don't know how to write a joke," says Ross. "Since most of my work is in full scripts, I just create funny characters and let them do the talking for me. *They* say funny things, not me. If you do your homework and have erected memorable and funny people, all you really need do is sit back and laugh as they speak cleverly to each other.

"One night, the late Allan Sherman and a psychiatrist-rabbi (believe it or not) and yours truly were embroiled in an argument over what single element was present in all humor. Allan opted for truth and said that in order to be funny, truth had to be present so the reader or viewer or listener could identify with it.

"The rabbi/shrink said hostility was the key. I'd have expected that from him, but I didn't know which side was speaking—the man of the cloth or the man of the couch.

"I felt the answer was surprise. Pat McCormick, a very funny man, has a way of combining inanimate objects with well-known people and making it work. For example: Pick up a large, clear, round glass ashtray. It could be a contact lens for the Jolly Green Giant. Or a bathtub for Mickey Rooney. Or the Statue of Liberty's diaphragm. None of those is true, and I don't see any serious hostility, but they are all surprises. Not necessarily funny, but surprises nonetheless." suggests Ross, who has received Emmy and Writers Guild nominations for "The Bill Cosby Show" and "All in the Family" segments.

"The same rules apply for writing a sketch as do in writing a half-hour script or even a comedy movie," points out Ross. "Get a cast of funny people (by that I mean funny characters, not the actors chosen), establish the conflict as fast as you can, and then do variations on it for the allotted time.

"Often you'll see a sketch on TV that ends with a lot of people running around. That's because they didn't know how to button it. Try to avoid that at all costs, because it's a cheat.

"Sometimes I know the punch line of the sketch before I know what precedes it. This is actually not a bad way to write. Start funny, get funnier, and finish funniest."

"Can you make any other specific suggestions?" I asked.

"Two basic sketch ideas you can use are the same ones Hitchcock used in his best dramatic films. The only difference is that he went for suspense and you are going for laughs. Take the ordinary person and put him in the extraordinary circumstance—like a priest who wanders by mistake into a massage parlor. Or do the opposite, the extraordinary person in the ordinary circumstance. Like the escaped ape who strolls into the PTA meeting.

"Now those two premises don't seem to be particularly sensational, but I could write two very funny sketches based on them. After you get the idea for your sketch or script, write a detailed outline of what's going to happen. Then, and *only* then, begin the dialogue.

"After finishing the work, put it away for anywhere from five minutes to five days, pull it out, and start cutting. Writing is rewriting, and don't ever forget it. When you've cut all the fat away, attack the meat. Then slash at the bone. When all you have is the marrow, and the marrow is hysterical, you've written a sketch."

Creating the Sitcom

When it comes to concocting an entire comedy series, a number of other components must be considered. It is one thing for a writer to fashion a segment for a successful sitcom already on the tube, quite another to start from scratch. Where do these new shows come from? How are they put together? What elements are necessary to make it succeed?

"The Beverly Hillbillies," on television for over nine years and still going strong in reruns, is a good example of a carefully constructed comedy series. Its creator, Paul Henning, tells how it came about:

"After five years of writing and producing 'The Bob Cummings Show' I took a fifteen-thousand-mile auto trip to historical sites in the U.S.A. After leaving Lincoln's cabin in Kentucky, I wondered what reaction Abraham Lincoln might have if he were transplanted from the nineteenth century and suddenly found himself seated in the car with me.

"I suppose I should preface all this by saying that I've always had a fondness for hillbilly humor," discloses Henning, who started in radio as a singer at KMBC, Kansas City, in 1933 and spent his early career writing for Fibber McGee and Molly, Rudy Vallee, and then George Burns and Gracie Allen. "As much as I loved Bing Crosby on his Kraft Music

Hall radio show, the highpoint for me was always the Bob Burns spot.

"Anyway, a few years after my trip, Al Simon urged me to create another TV series. I recalled my thinking about the fun of transplanting very unsophisticated rural folks into a completely opposite setting.

"Sudden wealth seemed the key to transplanting, so I established them in a tiny cabin in the remote hill country (no specific state), and had oil discovered on their property. Beverly Hills seemed the ideal posh community for them to move to, and it was close at hand for filming. Ergo, 'The Beverly Hillbillies.' "

Henning then had a meeting with Al Simon and Martin Rashohoff, who at that time was president of Filmways. Rashohoff agreed to finance the pilot. CBS saw it and bought it, and the show went on the air the following fall.

"How long did it take from concept to the first show actually being aired?" I asked Henning.

"About a year," he replied.

"Once you sold the show, what did you do to keep up the high quality of scripts?"

"I insisted on creative control and then wrote or co-wrote most of the almost three hundred scripts myself."

The show stayed in the top ten or twenty Nielsen ratings for its entire nine seasons.

"What were the key comedic ingredients that made the show a hit?" I asked.

"In my opinion any television show is based on characters," replied Henning. "If the audience doesn't like your characters, forget it! If you can put interesting and likable characters in funny situations, you've got it made. In the case of the Beverly

Hillbillies we had the added ingredient of their
being 'fish out of water.' "

The Producer

"Produced by" is one of the principal credits
listed at the end of every TV program. In the case of a
comedy series, very often the producer is also a
comedy writer who must dream up segments for the
show as well.

Some of the tube's best producers turn out to be
teams, men who have been associated together in
originating scripts. Among the top producers of hit
comedy series are Bill Persky and Sam Denoff
("Big Eddie," "Lotsa Luck"), Saul Turteltaub and
Bernie Orenstein ("Sanford and Son," "That Girl"),
Tom Patchett and Jay Tarses ("The Bob Newhart
Show"), Dave Davis and Lorenzo Music ("Rhoda"),
and Gene Reynolds and Larry Gelbart ("M*A*S*H").

But what is a producer? What is his function?
How does he contribute to the show? For what areas
is the producer responsible? What is his background?

Edwin Weinberger, producer of "The Mary
Tyler Moore Show," was a member of the "Tonight
Show" writing staff for five years. He not only wrote
jokes for Johnny Carson's opening monologue but
also hatched much of Johnny's nightclub material.

"The first step on 'The Mary Tyler Moore
Show,' " says Weinberger, "is to get a story idea for a
segment. So you work with various writers to come
up with one. If a writer comes into my office and he
has five ideas, one of which may be acceptable, then I
work with him to develop that idea. The producer
must approve the basic notion of the story.

"He then sees that story to its conclusion, even

after the original writer has left and gone on to write for another series," explains Weinberger, who got started in comedy by traveling for two years with and writing jokes for Dick Gregory. "So my first duty is to develop and deliver the best possible shooting script. Then there's casting, set decoration, checking wardrobe, music, overseeing practically everything that goes into the makeup of the show.

"Then while the show is being taped, the producer along with the director makes various decisions. Should we go back and do a scene over again? Could we do it in front of the audience? Should we wait until the audience goes home? Can we get away with that line? It even goes as far as saying, 'The studio's too hot. I think the audience'll laugh more if it's colder. Could we lower the temperature?'

"The producer's job covers that kind of minute detail all the way, even to what the star is going to wear," discloses Weinberger, who was also the story editor and cocreator of "The Bill Cosby Show." "Then in post-production, the producer works with the film editor to edit the show. You have to deliver the show to time. You shoot twenty-seven minutes; the show has to come in at twenty-three minutes. You have to take four minutes out. The producer is the one who decides what comes out, what stays in, whether to use a close-up for a certain shot or decide if it's best to show it from farther back.

"Television is a collaborative effort. The producer works in league with each department, each member of that department to see that the person does his job the best way possible..The producer coordinates all the parts, so that ultimately he is responsible for the entire show."

For Future Writers

Advice is seldom welcome; and those
who want it most always like it least.
Earl of Chesterfield, 1748

Since that learned gentleman never wanted to write comedy, he naturally wouldn't have been interested in suggestions on the best ways for a new writer to develop his talent. For those who may be looking for inside tips, the following counsel is offered by some of Hollywood's top professionals:

"If you want to be a good writer, you have to really like to write," says Stan Dreben, comedy contributor to Jackie Gleason, Milton Berle, Red Skelton, and an endless list of TV sitcoms. "You have to love comedy; you have to have a sensitivity, an awareness of what's going on. You have to be a student of human nature. You've got to read a lot of books on humor, see a lot of plays, movies, and comedy performers on television so that you know what's happening in the business. The routines, the trends!"

Paul Pumpian has provided gags for the Dean Martin TV roasts, Joey Bishop, Norm Crosby, Jack Carter, and others. "Lots of people say funny things now and then, but to be a professional you must be able to create a new joke on a moment's notice—or at least remember a related joke that will fit the occasion. Having a mind like this is a gift that one is born with and then nurtures over the years.

"I've been improving my comedy instincts for over twenty years, and by now I can honestly say that I'm one hell of a great writer," admits Pumpian. "If this sounds immodest, let me quote my ex-boss

Nat Hiken, who created "Sergeant Bilko" and "Car 54" during his career as a comedy writer and producer. Nat said, 'I wouldn't hire a man unless he felt sure that he was the funniest writer in the world. Every guy on my staff thinks he's the greatest, but, of course, they're all deluding themselves—because I am!' "

Lou Derman, head writer for "All in the Family" and a vast number of other TV sitcom segments, such as "I Love Lucy," "Mister Ed," "December Bride," "Life with Luigi," and so on, offers these thoughts:

"A man who just knows jokes is not going to make it writing for the top comedy series. He has to be a story writer. He should know the elements of play construction. Because he's basically writing a half-hour play every week which conforms to the rules of playwriting.

"The fact that it's funny happens to be a weird oddity. But it has a beginning, a middle, and an end. It has a first act climax and has a resolution at the end of the show, with a little point or some moral.

"He can learn the elements of playwriting from certain recognized books or take a course somewhere. When he's got the rules down, he can then use his comedy talent—a flair for the ridiculous—to bend the rules. And that makes him a comedy writer who's wanted, who can beat the competition and get jobs."

Mel Shavelson, another Bob Hope alumnus, has written a mountain of movie and TV scripts for most of the leading comedy performers.

"What does a young writer need? Rich parents!" quips Shavelson. "Comedy writing is a kind of controlled insanity. It's turning tragedy into comedy. The most important quality is originality. The true originals in humor go from Mark Twain to James Thurber to Woody Allen."

Is it possible to learn how to be an original?

"Yes," says Shavelson. "Originality can be cultivated by staying away from the obvious."

Perhaps the most prolific of all the TV scribes is J. Milton Josefsberg. He has served as writer and producer as well as script consultant to the industry's superstars: Bob Hope (seven years), Jack Benny (twelve years), Lucille Ball (eight years).

"A new writer would be wise to study one of the shows already on the air," counsels Josefsberg. "If you want to learn to write jokes, watch Mr. Hope. Record one of his monologues. Get it down on paper and then analyze it; notice how the jokes are constructed, the wording, the topics he uses.

"If situation comedy is what you want, take 'The Mary Tyler Moore Show' or whatever your favorite sitcom is—then study it. Understand the characters; see how the situation develops; and note how the humor springs from it. Then write your own. And keep doing it.

"The best advice is really in the form of an old joke:

> *A visitor to New York walked up to a newspaper stand and said to the dealer: 'How do I get to Carnegie Hall?'*
>
> *His reply was: 'Practice, mister! Practice!'"*